Eerie
DELAWARE

CHILLING TALES FROM
THE FIRST STATE

Josh Hitchens
Illustrations by Jason McLean

THE
History
PRESS

Published by The History Press
Charleston, SC
www.historypress.com

Front cover art by Jason McLean.

First published 2024

Manufactured in the United States

ISBN 9781467157452

Library of Congress Control Number: 2024931856

Notice: The information in this book is true and complete to the best of our knowledge. It is offered without guarantee on the part of the author or The History Press. The author and The History Press disclaim all liability in connection with the use of this book.

This book is dedicated in loving memory of
Brandi Nichole Eckler
May 9, 1988–November 2, 2021

She's the angel on top of the tree
And all the darling buds of May,
They fall with no sound.
—Courtney Love, "Petals"

and

for Carie Juettner,
for bringing The Ghostly Tales of Delaware to a younger generation

and

for Olive,
when you are old enough to read Uncle Josh's books.

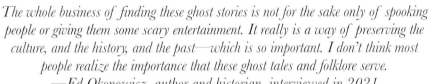

The whole business of finding these ghost stories is not for the sake only of spooking people or giving them some scary entertainment. It really is a way of preserving the culture, and the history, and the past—which is so important. I don't think most people realize the importance that these ghost tales and folklore serve.
—Ed Okonowicz, author and historian, interviewed in 2021

It is of some consolation to know, however, that if any people are deserving of a look ahead, behind the curtain and into the great unknown, it is the people of Delaware and the Eastern Shore.
—Morning News *of Wilmington, Delaware, October 6, 1881*

CONTENTS

Acknowledgements

N o one writes a book alone, and I have many people to thank for making the volume you hold in your hands a reality. First and foremost, there is Kate Jenkins and Ashley Hill, my editors at The History Press, who guided me through this process with consummate skill, support and patience. I would also like to thank Jason McLean for the beautifully evocative illustrations he provided for many of the chapters in this text. Your artistry enhances *Eerie Delaware* immeasurably, and I am eternally grateful for your invaluable contribution to this book.

   I am also immensely thankful for the assistance of many people and organizations who took the time to speak with me during the writing of this book, providing invaluable historical background and, in some cases, their own stories. You will find all their names throughout the following pages, but I would particularly like to thank Michael Connelly and everyone at the New Castle Historical Society and Kyle McMahon and the staff of Frightland. I would also like to give a very special thanks to Diane Flemming, who I met by chance at the Ebenezer Maxwell Mansion in Philadelphia. Upon seeing my book *Haunted History of Delaware* for sale there, she told me she was also from the First State and had lived in a haunted house for thirteen years. She kindly gave me her contact information and granted me an interview, in which she told me that rare thing: a ghost story that didn't take place over one hundred years ago. It was Diane telling me her incredible story that caused this book to be born, and for that, I am in her debt.

In collecting and retelling these tales, I stand on the shoulders of the historians and folklorists who have come before me. The Federal Writers' Project preserved an astonishing amount of folklore and history in its 1938 book *Delaware: A Guide to the First State*, an invaluable resource. Dorothy Williams Pepper devoted her life to recounting local legends and lore, most notably in her extraordinary 1976 book *Folklore of Sussex County, Delaware*. I must also pay tribute to the true giant of Delaware ghost stories: Ed Okonowicz. I can think of no other writer who has done more to document and preserve the creepy corners of the First State's history. He is a master storyteller, and I encourage everyone to seek out his substantial body of work. Other authors, including Mindie Burgoyne, Pam George, David Healey and Michael Morgan, have all written excellent books about the history and legends of the Eastern Shore, all published by The History Press, and I feel deeply honored to be in their company.

For residents of and visitors to the state of Delaware, I would like to encourage you to seek out the wonderful independent bookstores that do so much to support local authors like me. These stores include Hockessin BookShelf in New Castle County as well as Browseabout Books and Bethany Beach Books in Sussex County. All three are bookstores I've spent hours in since childhood, and it will never stop feeling surreal that my own books are now on their shelves.

I would like to thank my partner, Dr. Jacob Glickman, and my best friend, Ryan Walter, for assisting me in the research for *Eerie Delaware* and for giving me endless guidance and support. I would also like to thank Megan Edelman for reading the manuscript and providing invaluable feedback. Finally, I want to give the greatest thanks of all to my family, most of whom still live in southern Delaware and who have all never stopped believing in me and cheering me on when I have needed it most. This book and every book I write is inspired by and for all of you, with my deepest love.

Introduction

GATHER 'ROUND MY CAMPFIRE

Good evening, my friend. I have been waiting for you here, in the night, in the dark. Welcome to *Eerie Delaware: Chilling Tales from the First State*. If you have returned to my campfire after reading my first book, *Haunted History of Delaware*, or my second book, *Haunted History of Philadelphia*, I welcome you back. But if you have come to my campfire for the first time tonight, know that I am so pleased you found your way here. In fact, I have saved a very special place around my campfire just for you. I hope it is midnight wherever you are right now, for that is the best time of all to tell tales of terror. Imagine that it is the witching hour and turn the lights down low, as low as you can and still read these words. Sit with me here, in the shadows of this ancient, haunted forest, around these flickering flames. I have so many stories to tell you before the sun comes up. Come close to me and listen—if you dare.

My name is Josh Hitchens, and I tell ghost stories for a living. Since 2007, I have been a professional storyteller for the Ghost Tour of Philadelphia, the extremely historic and extremely haunted city I have lived in for twenty years as of this writing. However, the state of Delaware will always be the place I truly call home. I was born and raised in Sussex County. Branches of my family tree have lived in the state for centuries, as they still do today. A little country intersection within the woods of Sussex County is named Hitchens Crossroads in honor of my ancestors who made homes around there in times gone by. The Laurel Historical Society is currently restoring the Hitchens Homestead, a rural Gothic Revival cottage built in 1878 and occupied by six generations of my family, to become a local living history site and museum.

Growing up among the plentiful farmland and ever-present woods surrounding my childhood home and possessing a vivid imagination from an early age, I have always felt that Delaware's haunted history is extraordinarily present and alive. There are buildings standing silently in the forests that date back as far as the seventeenth century. Among the fields of corn, soybeans and chicken houses, you will sometimes find lonely, weed-choked family graveyards that have long been abandoned. And at night, as you drive in your car along the isolated, quiet country roads, you begin to wonder what strange things might be lurking behind the tall masses of trees, waiting for you in the dark.

When I was about eight years old, my grandparents took me on my first ghost tour. It was in Williamsburg, Virginia. Like Delaware, it is a perfect place for ghost stories, away from the modern world completely. It was pitch-black dark, except for the single white candle in the storyteller's lantern. She walked us through the fields and streets to the fronts of old landmarks. We could have been in any time. It could have been centuries ago. And as we listened to the ghost stories, told quietly in the night, we began to feel the tingling of fear start in the pit of our stomachs. Because, of course, there *are* ghosts in these houses, there *are* ghosts all around you, and at any second, you might see the apparition of a man running barefoot out of the woods, right toward you, coming for you. Then we looked at the windows of the deserted mansion, feeling absolutely certain that at any moment, we would see the face looking out at us—that terrible face we'd seen in our nightmares since we were young, something right in front of us that's been dead for a very long time. Sometimes, you never see the face. But sometimes, you do. By the end of that ghost tour, I knew what I wanted to do when I grew up. And here we are.

I take great pride in saying at the beginning of my ghost tour in Philadelphia, "I am not a paranormal investigator. I am a storyteller." I believe there is a great power in that, of knowing that I am part of a chain that goes back through the ages, ever since we learned to talk and sit around a fire, telling stories to each other in the dark. And ghost stories are always the best. When you feel truly afraid, you know you are alive. That moment when you are truly, deeply frightened can burn itself into your memory forever. Years later, you can recall every sensory detail, and you get the chill again and you shiver. That is what a ghost story can do—if the telling is good. The receiving and passing on of ghost stories and legends is, to me, the best and most enjoyable gateway to discovering the hidden riches of local history, no matter where you live.

"I saved a place around my campfire just for you."

One of the most formative experiences of my childhood was watching, every Saturday night at 9:30 p.m. on the Nickelodeon television channel, a horror anthology series for children and young adults called *Are You Afraid of the Dark?* Every weekend from 1992 to 1997, I was glued to my seat in front of the family television, watching thirty-minute tales of terror that are still with me decades later. Its opening credits alone are fuel for nightmares. The premise of the show is that a group of kids who call themselves the Midnight Society gather once a week in the woods around a blazing campfire. Then one of the members tells aloud a scary story they have written, which is then dramatized for the viewing audience. *Are You Afraid of the Dark?* was the brainchild of D.J. MacHale and Ned Kandel. In its very first episode, which was broadcast on Halloween night, the leader of the Midnight Society, Gary (played by Ross Hull), explained the nature and rules of this elite club that met weekly in the deep, dark woods, escaping from their parents, siblings, annoying school responsibilities and social cliques:

> *We're called the Midnight Society. Separately, we're very different. We like different things. We go to different schools, and we have different friends. But one thing draws us together—the dark. Each week, we gather around this fire to share our fears and our strange and scary tales. It's what got us together, and it's what keeps bringing us back. This is a warning to all who join us: You are going to leave the comfort of the light, and step into the world of the supernatural.*

As a young, spooky-minded boy who was never one of the popular kids, watching *Are You Afraid of the Dark?* every Saturday night was a revelation and a comfort, presenting the idea that the love of inventing and sharing scary stories could unite all of us in a moment of fright. No matter how different or weird you felt in the daytime at school, at night, in the dark, everyone could come together to experience and enjoy the telling of a scary tale. *Are You Afraid of the Dark?* still holds up incredibly well today, and to be truthful, it gave me my mission in life. You're sitting around my own campfire now, aren't you?

One of the great things about *Are You Afraid of the Dark?* was the immense variety of spooky stories it presented. There weren't just ghost stories, there were yarns about vampires, werewolves, witches, aliens, disturbing dolls, ghastly comic book characters that came to life and all manner of unearthly phenomena. You never knew what flavor of creepiness you were in for as the opening credits started every Saturday night. My first book, *Haunted History of Delaware*, consisted entirely of some of the First State's most famous haunted places. The only exception to this was a chapter about Patty Cannon, the first known female serial killer in the United States, who committed many heinous acts. That chapter was the only one in the book to have no supernatural elements at all. The truth of the history was horrific enough.

The book you are currently holding in your hands, *Eerie Delaware*, is a very different creature. You will find ghost stories here to be sure, tales of phantoms located in all corners of the state in extremely diverse places—historic mansions, museums, theaters, beaches and old hotels. We often think of old buildings being haunted, their stories handed down from over a century ago. But in this book, you will also find a tale of a haunting that occurred in recent years, told firsthand by the family who experienced the terror.

Aside from the ghost stories, you are also about to read stories of chilling urban legends and folklore that have scared generations of Delawareans. There are also tales of alien encounters from the nineteenth century to the present day that will make you watch the skies more closely at night. You will read of witchcraft and inhuman figures first experienced by the Lenni Lenape Native tribe thousands of years ago. Many say they are still lurking in the Delaware woods. This book also tells several harrowing tales of true crime that are still notorious, including an incident of cannibalism that occurred just off the Delaware coast, and of the First State's second known serial killer and the heroic efforts that finally brought an end to his bloody reign of terror. Finally, you will learn the fascinating history of Frightland, acclaimed as one of the best Halloween attractions in the United States. Frightland sends thousands of visitors screaming every October, but unlike most haunted attractions, it is haunted by real spirits from the land's tortured past.

Eerie Delaware contains all this and more, and even still, I know I am only just scratching the surface of the weird and wonderful tales my home state has to offer. Whether you are reading this book while relaxing on one of our beaches or cozily in your bed at home, wherever that may be, I hope you enjoy these chilling stories. Savor them one or two at a time, and then perhaps tell your favorites to your friends or your family on some dark and stormy night after turning out all the lights. By telling these stories to others in your own way, you are playing an important part in keeping the immensely rich history—and the oftentimes frightening folklore—of Delaware alive for many generations to come. Tell these tales. Pass them on in the night, in the dark.

I wish you happy reading and pleasant dreams.

1

A Haunted House in Hockessin

When we think of haunted houses, we often imagine decaying and fearsome structures that were built centuries ago, places that look like all manner of ghosts and ghouls inhabited them from the very beginning. The lawns are overgrown and uncared for; the paint of the cursed homes has been slowly peeled away to ragged shreds by time; their rooms are filled with moth-eaten antique furniture, long abandoned after some horrific tragedy took place; and ideally, they have an old graveyard populated by crooked tombstones somewhere close by, revealing the homes' spooky secrets.

Sometimes, haunted houses are like that. Delaware boasts several of them. But sometimes, there is a haunted house that defies the creepy pictures we have created in our minds, a house that looks much like the one you may have grown up in. These are modern-looking houses that stand alone along a main road, seemingly normal and ordinary, but in fact, they are extremely haunted. In the town of Hockessin, Delaware, located in New Castle County, you will find such a house.

What is now known as the town of Hockessin came into existence in 1688, when a few brave families decided to make their homes there. There are two different folkloric origins of the name of this small community. One says that the town's name was drawn from the Native tribe the Lenni Lenape, who occupied the land for thousands of years before it was named Delaware. Their word *hoke* means "good bark," or "the place of many foxes." But there is also another possible origin story for that town's name that is borne out by the historical record.

According to the 1938 book *Delaware: A Guide to the First State*, by the Federal Writers' Project, "The tract where Hockessin stands was part of Letitia Manor, a 15,000-acre estate given by William Penn to his daughter Letitia in 1701, which was then broken up and sold to settlers." Originally, the area known as Hockessin was called Mill Creek Hundred by its white colonists and was subsequently renamed Occasion by William Cox in 1734 in a deed for his property. The road leading to the Quaker meetinghouse was, in 1808, noted as Ockessian Road, which may have led to the town's contemporary name.

In 2021, I gave a tour of the Ebenezer Maxwell Mansion, the only Victorian house museum in Philadelphia (sadly not haunted); one of the people on the tour was a woman named Diane Flemming. She saw my book *Haunted History of Delaware* on display, and after the tour was over, she told me she had lived in a haunted house in Delaware for thirteen years. I shared that I was beginning to write the book you are reading now and asked if she would be willing to tell me the story of what she had experienced at her haunted house in Hockessin.

This tale includes mentions of domestic violence and alcoholism. What you are about to read is Diane Flemming's terrifying account of a contemporary haunting, told in her own words.

The house was on a main road. It was secluded, actually. I didn't have any neighbors next to me. I had a neighbor behind me, and I had a nursing home across the street from me, and that was about it. When I first bought the house, there was a house next to me, but they tore it down before I moved in, so there were really no neighbors, really. It was a brick house, painted white. I guess you could call it a Colonial style. But I painted the shutters and the doors red. I think they were black when I first bought it. And it had a bedroom that was later added, and it had a detached garage and an enclosed porch. And I had a cottage on the property as well. I'd rent it out. And at one point, my daughter and her boyfriend and my grandson were living in there.

I think the house was built around the 1940s. I was actually the first non–family member that ever lived there. I made settlement on the house December 31, 1999. After I moved in, when I first moved in, my husband and I noticed the smell of perfume. But it seemed to be like an older lady's perfume; it wasn't like a modern perfume. And it just permeated the whole downstairs, upstairs. But then I would go in my room and come back out, and it would be gone. So, it was really weird that it would come and go like

"The house was on a main road." *Photograph by Cschroeder999, Wikimedia Commons.*

that. The whole time we lived in the house, there was a room upstairs that used to be the bedroom of the couple that lived there, and there was a little closet—my daughter and I called it the Anne Frank closet—and it always smelled like that perfume. For thirteen years.

That was the first thing.

And then we had a dog; it was a little miniature poodle. My husband at the time hung up a painting, a picture on the wall, and the dog constantly barked at that wall. Constantly. And finally, the picture fell, and I found out later when my house went on fire and the cars in the driveway went on fire— one of the firefighters said, "You know, that house, that front room, that's where the old man's deathbed was. I carried him out of there when he died."

I found out a lot about the people who lived there. The [husband]—I don't know if he was a corporal, but he was someone higher up in the Delaware State Police. Apparently, he was not a nice man. [His wife] drank, and he beat her. There used to be a bar around the corner, and she'd sneak out at night and go to the bar, and he'd get her in the alleyway by the house, and he'd beat her.

There were times…one time I had a tenant over at the cottage and she said to me the next day, and I heard it, too, she said to me, "Did you hear the whispering out in the alleyway last night?" And I said, "Yeah, I did. I

19

heard people whispering out there." I went out to set the heat, and I heard all kinds of whispering. Apparently, he used to beat her out there. I had one tenant come and look at the cottage, and I guess she was an empath or something, and she said, "I cannot go near that alleyway. Bad stuff happened out there." She never rented the place because of that.

And the guy who lived behind me told me that [the wife who lived in the house said to her abusive husband,] "If I die first, I'm coming back to haunt you." Apparently [the husband] slept in different rooms every night because he was afraid she was going to come back and get him after she died.

The room where the closet was, which was turned into my daughter's room, that was their bedroom originally. But they added a second bedroom as they got older because it was on the first floor, and that was where my room was. And apparently, the wife died in that room. I'm going to tell you a story about my grandson, who was only about two and half years old at the time, and he comes up to me one day, and he said, "Mommom, that old lady tried to pick me up." And I said, "Did somebody come into your daycare and try to pick you up?" And he goes, "No, that old lady in your bedroom picked me up."

So, after a while, I started talking to her, telling her I would take care of her house, because, like I said, I was the first non–family member to ever live in that house. I just think she was there the whole time. One time, my husband went golfing down the street at the country club, and he was saying to people, "I just moved into the area. I live in that house." And they all said, "You know that house is haunted." And they said that the kids in the '70s used to go by and look for ghosts.

One time, my daughter was in the shower upstairs—she was pregnant with my grandson—and she said she shut the water off, and all of a sudden, she heard this loud commotion going on downstairs. On my dining room table at the time, I had these plastic plate chargers, you know, that you put the plates on; I had four of them. And I had a bunch of flowers in the middle. And my daughter said she came down and every one of the place settings were upside down in each chair, but the flowers were still there in the middle. She called me and said, "Ma, I can't stay here."

I rented the upstairs room a couple times after my daughter moved into the cottage. And one time, my tenant came down and she said, "Diane, did you come into my room last night?" And I said, "No, why?" And she said, "Because the door opened, and someone was standing there. And I was awake."

"She was going to come back."

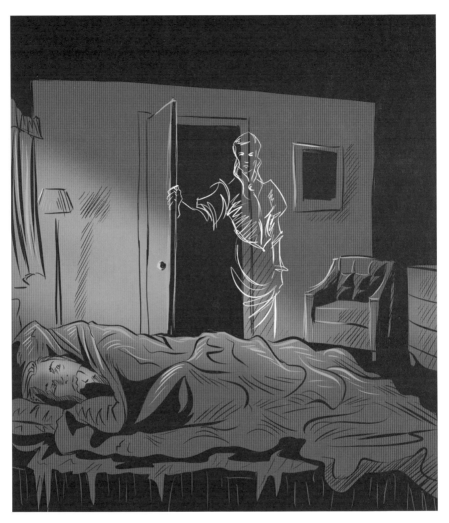

"Someone was standing there."

Later, I rented it to another guy who had a little boy, and I ran into him at the store after he moved out. And he said, "I don't know how to tell you this, but that house is haunted." Of course I knew! I said, "What makes you say that?" He said, "My son would never stay in that room by himself because he said that old man was in there."

Another time, a friend of mine was painting the house, and she called me while I was at work, and she said, "I don't know what's going on here, but I gotta leave." She didn't know about the house. She said, "I gotta leave. I feel like somebody is standing over me. Because the hair on the back of my

neck is standing up, and I don't feel good at all in this house. I've gotta go."
I just got so used to it.

I don't think the wife was happy in that house. I had the feeling she used to hide in that little closet, maybe to get away from her husband, and that's why the perfume was always strongest there. The guy who lived behind me said that the police would never come. Because of who the husband was in the state police, they would never come out. So, I don't think she had a very good life. That's why she used to sneak out and drink a lot, and I can't blame her. After she died, they built the cottage just for the husband, and the rest of the family moved into the big house. Eventually, he got Parkinson's.

Stuff happened in the cottage, too. I had a couple people in there tell me that weird things were happening. When my daughter and her boyfriend moved in there, the boyfriend had this decorative sword in a sheath, and it was up on top of a dresser in their bedroom. They woke up one morning, and the sword was in the living room, out of its sheath, and the sword and sheath were laying side by side on the floor.

Also, one time, they thought they heard someone on the steps, and it was in the snow. They thought they heard someone rattling the door, trying to get in. When they opened the door and went out, they saw bare footprints in the snow leading up to the door, but nobody was there. So, both the house and the cottage had stuff going on.

I used to have another girl that lived in the cottage, and she would tell me weird stuff she would hear going on. That alleyway—we were always hearing stuff in that alleyway. All you could hear was whispering. You couldn't tell if it was male or female voices. I never saw anything, but I just knew. I knew she was there. I think that it was her house, and she wasn't ready to leave. And I would tell her all the time, "I'm taking good care of your house."

But my dog, that little dog, for the longest time, at three o'clock in the morning, would bark out the side window into that alleyway. And I know it's like three o'clock, it's like the witching hour, whenever there's a paranormal something, it's always at three o'clock. But my daughter would wake up all the time around three o'clock and say, "That dog just keeps barking and barking at that alleyway. Something's out there, something's out there." And she'd look, and nothing would be there.

I had other things happen that were not paranormal, like my ex-husband tried to burn the house down. It was always just not good things there. I bought the house, and I got divorced, and he tried to pay somebody to burn it down. Two cars were on fire in the driveway, the garage was on fire, trees *were on fire. I lived there for thirteen years, and I guess I kind of got used to it, but people would come in and be like, "There's something in this house." They didn't even know about it; they were just like, "I get bad vibes in here, and I don't know what it is."*

But I was never afraid. I was never afraid, because I really thought it was her. It was her house, and she just wasn't ready to leave. I never got an idea of him, *it was always* her *and that perfume. It wasn't evil, it wasn't mean; she never did anything mean. I would find things in different places than I'd thought I'd put them, but that could have been me. A lot of times I'd say, "I swear I put this thing here, and now it's somewhere else."*

About three months ago, I pulled up in the driveway of the house, and the people I sold it to were outside. I was talking to them and asked them how they liked it there and stuff, and they—they kind of got quiet. And I said, "Is something going on? Because I think this place has somebody in it." And one of the guys started yelling, "Mom! Mom! It's true! It's true!" Then he goes, "Just the other night, we had a case of beer on the kitchen counter, and it was full. Then we went into the living room, and we came back, and one of the cans was out. It was sitting on the countertop." And the wife drank—she was a drinker. They said there were other things going on in there, too. So, there's definitely something in that house.

This was one other weird thing. When I first moved in, the one bedroom that looked out to the alleyway had a lock on the outside *of the door. Like there was something in there they didn't want to get out. But like I said, I never felt threatened because I assumed it was her. I lived with it, and she lived with me. She just did a few things, like picking up my grandson!*

My grandson was so little at the time, and when he said that to me, I thought, "Oh, Jesus," you know? He also told me—you know how kids are, they're very in tune with this stuff, I think. His great-grandmother died the day before he was born. So, he never knew her. And one night, he was in the tub, making bubbles with his mouth in the water, and I said, "How'd you learn how to do that?" And he said—he was only like two—he said, "Shirley taught me." Shirley was the name of his great-grandmother that died the day before he was born.

So, the next time you find yourself driving through Delaware on a quest to find the eerie places and corners of the state, slow down and look at the houses you pass. You might see a house in Hockessin that doesn't look like a haunted house. It looks like any other house you might see on the roads you travel along on your journey. But this house, this ordinary-looking house, is haunted.

"Shirley taught me."

Diane's story is also an important reminder that not all ghosts are scary. Sometimes, they can be the spirit of a loving, departed family member, reaching out from the beyond for a moment to teach their now-two-year-old great-grandchild how to blow bubbles in the bathwater for fun.

2

BEWARE OF WITCHES IN THE WOODS

The woods of Delaware are numerous, dark and deep. And in those woods, among the tall trees, lurk many a frightening thing. If you dare to explore these forests, make sure you wear bright colors to make yourself known to any hunters who might be nearby. But there are some regions among the trees of the First State where no hunter dares venture. They will have heard the legends, of course, and they know to avoid these areas—or else they might disappear and never be seen alive again.

These wooded regions of Delaware are occupied by unearthly creatures that have been known to the Lenni Lenape Native tribe for thousands of years. One of these beings is called the Pukwudgie, which means "little man of the woods who vanishes." The Pukwudgie is found in only two places in the world: Prince Edward Island in Canada and Sussex County, Delaware. They appear to lost travelers in the woods as creatures that are only two or three feet tall. They appear human from the front, but on their backs, they have the deadly quills of a porcupine. According to Native legend, the Pukwudgies were friendly to humans at first but then turned against them. If you encounter the Pukwudgies' wrath, they will hunt you in the forest. They can disappear and shapeshift. They create fire using their magic and can blind you with sand and erase your memories. They will finally entice you to jump off a high hill and then feast on your flesh and bones.

Another legendary creature of Lenni Lenape folklore that was once said to haunt the Delaware woods is the terrifying Mhuwe. Similar to the Native tales of the Wendigo, the Mhuwe was described as an ice giant,

Beware the Pukwudgie.

once a human being, who was driven insane by starvation and was finally compelled to commit the ultimate evil of consuming human flesh. After this act, the person was transformed into the monstrous giant Mhuwe creature and now roams the woods, looking for more victims. In Lenni Lenape lore, a Mhuwe who is treated kindly and given food of the nonhuman variety can be transformed back into a human being—so the legend says.

The Delaware woods are also known for their tales of witches. One of these witches haunts a region known as the "Wedge" in New Castle County. The Wedge is a 1,068-square-mile piece of land that sits along the borders of Delaware, Maryland and Pennsylvania. The ownership of this piece of land was disputed for many years before it was finally awarded to the State of Delaware in 1921. On April 1, 2021, the official New Castle County Twitter account posted: "Per the terms of our 100-year rental agreement with Pennsylvania, we're returning the Wedge to our neighbors to the north today." It was, of course, an April Fool's joke. But the witch of the Wedge is no joke.

Her legend was recorded by noted Delaware author and folklorist Ed Okonowicz in *Presence in the Parlor*, the fifth book in his incredible Spirits Between the Bays series that documents the hauntings and eerie occurrences of the Eastern Shore. The following is what he said about the terrifying legend of the witch of the Wedge, who is, in many ways, the First State's version of *The Blair Witch Project*:

> *Her name is Melinda. That's what people say, anyway.….No one wanted to go into the Wedge, not even the police. Too many who had wandered into its forests and gullies didn't come out. Hunters never made it home. Travelers who tried to take the shortcut never arrived at their destinations. Children who wandered off, ignoring their parent's warnings, became the "lost children" of the Wedge. When that happened, the old folks would whisper the name, "Melinda." "It's the work of the Witch of the Wedge," or "I hear she got another one," they'd say.*
>
> *It is impossible to find out the origin of Melinda's existence. Folklore files in the local libraries, old newspaper editions and area history books make passing references to disappearances in the Wedge, but there is no specific mention of Melinda. After interviews with several old-timers, those few who would talk at all…while none of these stories could be confirmed, in the 1890s there were reports of an old woman, dressed in a tattered black cape. Spotted infrequently at the edge of the forest picking berries, she was seen in the company of animals. When approached or*

called to, she disappeared into the brush. Tales of the Witch of the Wedge continued over the years.

At the turn of the century, several trespassers into the thick woods disappeared, especially those who went in alone, and definitely anyone who was stupid enough to enter the woods of the Wedge at night. When fishermen along the White Clay Creek would not return, their boots were found at the spot they were last seen, but no other clue as to their whereabouts was discovered. No tracks leading away. No trails or broken brush. Absolutely no clues. Nothing. Anyone separated from his mates in the search party would suffer a similar fate. Only a pair of empty shoes or boots was left behind. Folks figured these were warnings not to come any farther.

Even children were not spared. In the 1920s, a gang of young boys thought that a midnight search for Melinda would be a proper initiation for the new members wanting to join their club. Within an hour of their trip to the Wedge, three of the seven children disappeared. A few days later, three pairs of tiny shoes were found near the creek bed, close to where it now meets the bridge on Hopkins Road. The club disbanded quickly, due to lack of membership. To no one's surprise, trips into the dense brush of the Wedge ceased for many years. Even police, parents, and officials declined to pursue the search for any of the missing.

"Only a pair of empty shoes or boots was left behind."

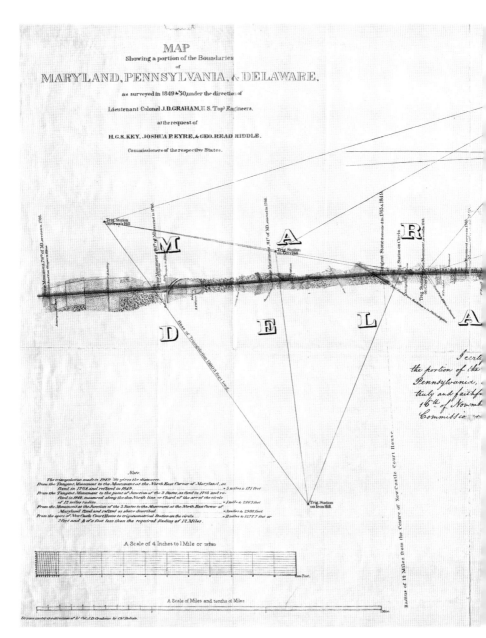

A map showing a portion of the boundaries of Maryland, Pennsylvania and Delaware as surveyed in 1849 and 1850. At this time, the "Wedge" was still considered part of Pennsylvania. *Public domain.*

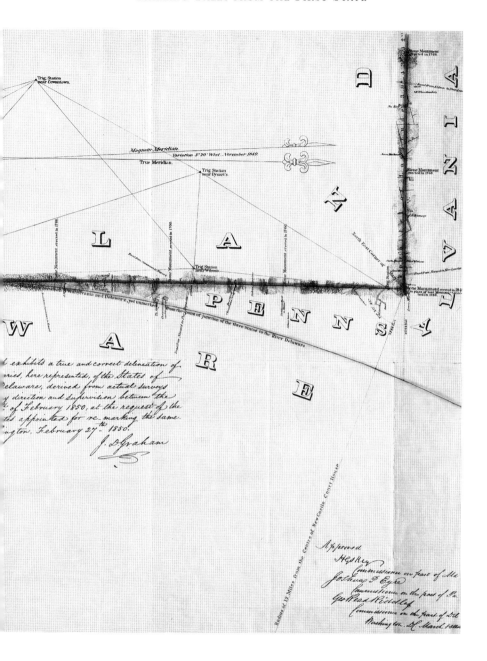

But of course, some people never learn. Human beings often do reckless things in the name of greed, and so it was in the 1930s, when rumors spread that there was a fortune in pirate treasure buried deep in the woods of the Wedge. This was the time of the Great Depression, and many were poor. The allure of potential gold was enough to make a group of men forget the tales of the witch and the many disappearances that had occurred in the area during the previous decades. "Superstitious nonsense," they said. So, one dark night, they ventured into Melinda's territory in search of a great fortune. A group of thirteen men went into the woods that night, all led by a man named Red, who swore up and down that he knew the exact location of the buried treasure.

It wasn't long before they became lost in the woods of the Wedge. Red cursed and mumbled that his compass was broken; the needle kept going around and around like the hands of a clock. And then, out of the pitch-black darkness, the men heard a voice call out to them. It was the horrible voice of an ancient, grotesque hag, piercing through the night as if gurgling from an open grave: "Leave this place! Leave this place! Or you will all die!"

At first, there was silence. Then the thirteen men began to laugh, asking each other, "Which one of you fellas did the voice of the witch? That was a good one—you got me there for me minute!" But no one admitted to doing the voice. And then the forest surrounding them began to fill with sounds. They all raised their rifles, but it was too late. Suddenly, all the animals of the forest were upon them. Deer gored men with their antlers. Possums and squirrels and spiders dropped from the trees above them, attaching themselves to the men's tender necks, clawing them and drinking their blood. Their screams echoed for miles outside of the Wedge. All the neighbors heard them. But they shut their windows, locked their doors and turned out all the lights. They knew better than to interfere with the witch's revenge.

The next morning, Red was found at the edge of the woods; he was wounded but still alive. Surrounding him, in a perfect circle, were twelve pairs of shoes. The men they had belonged to were never seen again, and their bodies were never found. The old-timers say that Red was committed to an asylum for the incurably insane for the rest of his life. He was kept there for the rest of his days in a straitjacket. He never stopped screaming about the old witch and her burning eyes.

———•———

Another famous Delaware legend is that of the Witch's Tree. Supposed in folklore to be located near the Sussex County town of Selbyville, it is a dark and twisted tree where a witch was hanged in times gone by. It is still thought to be haunted and possess supernatural power, and it is supposedly a site for contemporary occult rituals. Its story says that unexplained lights and orbs are found near the tree at night and that if you dare to seek out its location, you will be chased away by a black pickup truck that is parked near it in the woods. The unexplained thing is that the woods around the Witch's Tree have no roads, so it is impossible for a truck to have been there. But it is there, and many a brave seeker has been driven away from this fearsome place at night. Many people who have been to the site have heard the sounds of a woman screaming in terror. It is not uncommon for those who seek the Witch's Tree to have their vehicles break down and refuse to start, leaving them alone in the darkness of the woods.

Authors Mark Sarro and Gerald J. Medvec, in writing their book *Ghosts of Delaware*, went on a quest to find the Witch's Tree. They went to the local libraries of Selbyville and nearby towns; they asked the local historians. None of them knew anything about the Witch's Tree, so Sarro and Medvec concluded that the Witch's Tree did not exist.

But the Witch's Tree does exist. The problem is that it is not actually located in Delaware; it is a ten-minute drive southwest of Selbyville in the woods of Whaleyville, Maryland. It's close enough to be a part of this book's folklore, I'd say. In the old times, the borders between Delaware and Maryland were arbitrary and often fiercely debated. Regardless, the Witch's Tree did stand there, gnarled and uncanny. Mindie Burgoyne, the author of *Haunted Eastern Shore* and many other excellent spooky books about the region, posted a picture of the tree on her *Chesapeake Ghosts* Facebook page in 2015, saying, "Finally found it. And the energy around this tree is palpable."

Dr. Carol A. Pollio, who is a psychic, also found the Witch's Tree and wrote about her experiences on her website www.intuitive-investigations.com:

A few years ago, on Halloween, I wanted to do something different (and paranormal). I decided to visit the Witch's Tree in Whaleyville, MD, near the southern Delaware border. The tree is located off the beaten path a bit and is technically within the Great Cypress Swamp, a conservation area managed by Delaware Wild Lands....As a biologist, I found it to be an amazing tree. It is a large chestnut oak (not a bald cypress, as some sites have claimed) and appeared to have been a witness tree. Witness trees were once used to mark property when the site was not suitable for a traditional marker.…In this case, the surrounding forest is much younger and contains a wider variety of species than the original forest would have had. Because of these younger trees, the Witch's Tree really is notable—it is larger, taller, and more gnarled than any others in that area.…It is definitely a foreboding area and one I wouldn't want to visit on a pitch dark night (though I probably will!). The gnarls on the tree and its many broken and dead branches also add to its off-putting silhouette—I can definitely see where it would make people uncomfortable.…As I touched it back then, I did feel something unusual. It felt like a deep sorrow.…There is definitely something to the folklore about this tree.…It demanded your respect—it had presence, if you will.

The Witch's Tree, so close to Selbyville, Delaware, has inspired its own origin story. Whether this is the truth or merely legend is not known. But the following tale has been posted on the internet as a Creepypasta by a user named Gripping Fear:

There has been a legend going on in our town, a legend that dates back all the way to the colonial times, a legend that involves a woman by the name of Allison Gregory. Allison was a woman who lived in a small village in Delaware during the late colonial era. It was a peaceful, quiet town. Everybody just lived a normal life. Nobody really knew Allison, she was usually such a quiet woman, she never really got involved in social affairs or anything like that. Normally, she was practically a shut-in, she would just stay in her house and not go out, she never really had any friends. Now during this time, there was already paranoia of witches and evil forces, which caused people to kill many innocents out of fear.

One day, there was a knock on Allison's door. When she opened it, it was a messenger from another town. He told her news that her sister, who lived in that town, was accused of being a witch and killed. Allison was dumbfounded; she could not believe what she had heard. For days she would mourn for her lost sister. Then one day, she stopped mourning. She was not heard from for months.

It was during these months where the town fell into chaos. There was famine, citizens falling ill, deaths in the mayor's family.…When Whaleyville's village heard of this, they knew that it must have been her, Allison Gregory, and they knew that she did it for revenge.

They broke down her door to find her in the basement. She looked awful, ragged, she shook violently as her beady eyes looked at the mob. The villagers

The Witch's Tree.

noticed that there were all different types of liquids and jars of powder on her shelves. Two people then charged at Allison, they knocked her to the ground, she fell unconscious.

The mob carried Allison into the forest, the night was cold and dark. In the forest, they found a tree, its branches bare, its bark was black, it looked as if no life was in it. They took another rope and tied her to the tree, Allison screamed and struggled with no avail. The local priest came up to her, he carried a blessed dagger. He held it up to the sky and chanted holy words. When the chanting was over, the priest raised the dagger and stabbed her through the heart. Allison Gregory died screaming.

Today, there is a legend saying that since the tree had no life in it, the ghost of Allison went into the tree. The tree is now called The Witch's Tree, and anybody that says this chant will free her spirit.

Witch's soul,
Now lost forever.
I now summon you,
Allison Gregor.

This is only a legend. Of course it is. And if truth be told, sadly, just a few years ago, the real Witch's Tree was cut down—no one knows why. Only its mutilated stump exists today, still scarred with spraypainted occult symbols. But it remains a sacred place, where those who dare to invoke the witch gather on nights of the full moon. Beware. Beware.

3

CANNIBALISM OFF THE DELAWARE COAST

The sea—the sound of the waves, the smell of salt water, the feeling of being gently cradled by the eternal up-and-down rhythm of the ocean— is a source of relaxation and joy for many of us, me included. Take a ride on the Cape May–Lewes Ferry, and you can experience it for yourself. The Lewes side is known to be haunted by the multitude of drowned sailors who were buried in a mass grave beneath its modern parking lot, as I recounted in my first book, *Haunted History of Delaware*. The sea can be comforting, as all those who live along the coast of the First State can attest. But just imagine now if you were out on the water on a small boat during a raging storm in the dead of winter. Imagine that you are drifting far away from the ship you call home, into the vast, unforgiving waters of the Atlantic Ocean with no fresh water, no food, no warm clothes, no compass, no way to get back to safety. What would you do to survive?

During a dark and turbulent November storm in 1884, three men, pilot Marshall Bertrand and his apprentices Andreas Hansen and Alfred Swanson, were forced to answer that question. All three were sailors on the *Enoch Turley* and were charged with taking a skiff (a shallow, flat-bottomed, open boat with a sharp bow and square stern) to deliver pilot Thomas Marshall to a ship called the *Pennsylvania*. It was November 22, 1884, when the three sailors embarked on this task, and despite the high winds and churning waters, they succeeded in delivering Marshall to the safety of the *Pennsylvania* just off the coast of Cape Henlopen around 5:00 a.m. However, during their return voyage in the dark to their home ship, *Enoch Turley*, things began to go very wrong.

"The winds raged, and the waves of the sea rose."

The winter storm they had set out in had worsened considerably. The winds raged, and the waves of the sea rose so high that they feared their small boat might capsize. But what was worse was that the three men, Marshall Bertrand, Andreas Hansen and Alfred Swanson, suddenly realized that they could no longer see the *Enoch Turley* as they drifted farther out into the Atlantic Ocean. And what was even worse: they could no longer see the beams of the Delaware lighthouses, meaning they were far away from finding shelter and at the mercy of the unforgiving sea during a severe winter storm. At the same time, the crew of the *Enoch Turley* also lost sight of the men's small boat and began searching for them, a search that encompassed three hundred miles of the Delaware coast. But with such bad weather, it was supposed by the crew of the *Enoch Turley* that Bertrand, Hansen and Swanson had gone down to Davy Jones's locker and were resting at the bottom of the ocean's deep abyss. The *Delaware Gazette and State Journal* newspaper reported that the three men were missing and presumed dead.

But they were not dead—not yet. And if Marshall Bertrand, Andreas Hansen and Alfred Swanson had known the crew of the *Enoch Turley* and other ships were searching for them, they would not have been comforted much. All three men had set off on their mission in the early morning hours of Monday, November 22, 1884, with the expectation that their time away from their home ship to deliver the pilot would be a quick one, as these trips routinely were. Therefore, they had not dressed themselves for long-term exposure to the intense cold and wetness of a winter storm. They had taken with them no provisions—no food, no water. They were completely unprepared for surviving alone in a storm in a small boat.

Marshall Bertrand, the most experienced sailor of the three, took the helm of their small skiff, while Hansen and Swanson took turns bailing out the water that began pooling in the vessel and threatened to sink them all. As the *New York Times* later reported: "Soon the spray, driven by the cutting blasts, froze upon their oilskins, and their stiffened muscles failed to do their duty." But on that Monday afternoon, Andreas Hansen later told a tale of how they saw approaching ships and were twice almost rescued from their terrible plight:

> *We could see the boat plainly and also the light ship at Five Fathom bank, but the pilot boat did not see us and the harder we rowed for her the faster she went from us. We halloed and signaled, but to no avail, as the boat did not see us, and appeared to be trying to get away from us. We gave up the chase for the pilot boat and tried to make the lightship, but the wind was so strong against us that we could not make any headway. About 3 o'clock we saw a bark, supposed to be the* Viator. *We rowed to her and were within a line's throw. We asked the captain to take us aboard, and he merely waved his hand in a negative manner. We asked him for water, and he refused. We asked him for a piece of hard bread, and he refused. The captain then squared his sails and left us.*

After this incident, Marshall Bertrand bitterly screamed a dire curse at the ship sailing away from them: "By God, I hope you'll sink before sunset!" Bertrand continued his narrative:

> *All Monday, and Monday night, we drove aimlessly about, suffering the extremes of hunger, thirst, and cold. Towards dusk on Monday evening, the other men* [Hansen and Swanson], *who were pilot apprentices, became delirious. And, before I could control them, they threw overboard the oars and everything else that was loose in the boat. Thus, left without any means of handling the skiff, I can hardly explain how it escaped filling or capsizing. I occasionally sunk into a stupor, in which the ravings of my shipmates, the roar of the wind, and the lashing of the waves, were furiously mingled in whatever remained to me of consciousness.*

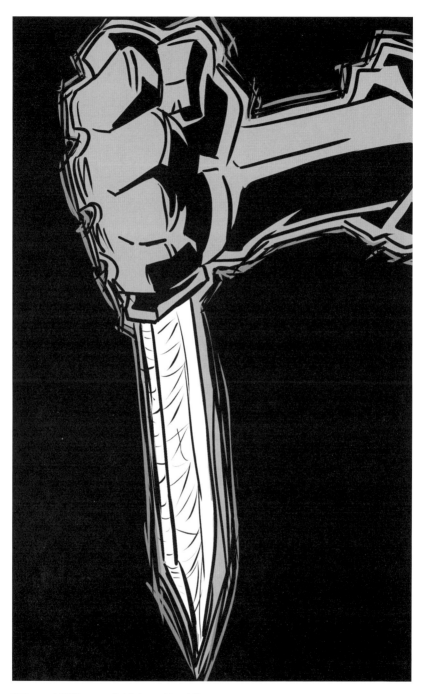

"He would kill me and drink my blood."

I suppose that it was about midnight of Monday when Swanson drew his sailor's knife from its sheath and made several plunges at me, declaring that he would kill me and drink my blood. Although roused to consciousness by this danger, I was too weak to make any resistance, and, closing my eyes, patiently waited for death, that seemed near and not unwelcome. But the deranged man was himself too feeble to carry out his intention. Exhausted by his long fast and clad in his icy garments, he fell, shrieking and gasping, at my feet. In a few minutes he was dead. The clouds had passed away, the moon had risen, and its beams fell upon the contorted features of the dead sailor, upon whose face the freezing spume-drift quickly formed a film of ice. To add to the peril…the boat shipped a great deal of water. The bailer was among the things that the crazy men had thrown overboard, and I was forced to take off one of my rubber boots to use in its place. Thus I freed the boat from water, but my unprotected foot was frozen. Hansen was so near death as to be incapable of rendering any assistance. And, except when he was raving, he laid like a log.

This was Marshall Bertrand's version of what happened. But Andreas Hansen told his own story, which was similar but also contradictory to Bertrand's in ways that should be noticed:

As darkness came on Monday night it was extremely cold, and we all lay down to sleep. The pilot [Bertrand] and I were in the stern of the boat and Swanson in the bow. We had not been down long before Swanson unsheathed a large knife and began to sharpen it. The pilot got up, went to him, and asked what he was going to do, and he said: "I am going to cut you to get some blood." The pilot said: "It is no use for you to cut me," and then took the knife from him. Meanwhile Swanson was crazy, and, being angered, he threw all the oars overboard. I went to sleep, and when I awoke Tuesday morning, I saw Swanson dead in the boat.

A reporter for the *New York Times* then asked Andreas Hansen if he had seen Alfred Swanson die. Hansen replied, "No. I know nothing about it." Marshall Bertrand said that both Andreas Hansen and Alfred Swanson had gone temporarily insane at this point, although Hansen had his own vivid recollections of that time. The central question, which can never be fully answered, is how did Alfred Swanson die that night? Did he suddenly expire after he declared he wanted to kill Marshall Bertrand and drink his blood, or was he perhaps murdered in justifiable self-defense?

We will never know. Hansen, the only other living witness, "knew nothing about it."

Andreas Hansen continued his narrative:

> *The weather was quite fair on Tuesday. The pilot* [Bertrand] *tore up the inside planks and made oars and a mast, to which he attached clothing for sails. We sailed all day Tuesday, and we were both very thirsty and hungry. Tuesday night was very fine; the moon was up and very bright, and it shone down upon us, and into the glistening and glaring eyes of our dead companion.*

Marshall Bertrand and Andreas Hansen had now survived forty-eight hours without any food, water or appropriate clothing to shield them from the chill of winter as they were lost on the sea. Marshall Bertrand related what happened next as Wednesday, their third day, dawned:

> *When the sun rose on Wednesday morning, I eagerly scanned the horizon in search of a sail, but I saw nothing. As my glance fell upon the corpse of the dead sailor, it occurred to me that he might be the means of prolonging life until rescue came. Horrible as the idea of cannibalism was to me, I realized that nothing else remained between me and death. I roused Hansen and was happy to discover that his mind had comparatively cleared, and that he understood what was said to him. The cold had not abated, but the sea had gone down, the day was bright, and I knew that if we could keep alive until nightfall, we would in all likelihood be picked up, as we could not be out of the path of the coasting vessels. Then came the supreme moment when I indicated to Hansen what I proposed to do, and the latter agreed with me. With the small remnant of strength left us we tore the stiffened oilskins and the underclothing from the dead and left a portion of the body exposed. Into his breast and shoulders we plunged our knives and eagerly sucked the blood from the wounds. We immediately felt refreshed and the tortures which we had experienced were allayed. Pausing for a moment in our work, we returned to it and cut strips of flesh from the corpse. Each devoured a little, with a loathing which only the conviction of self-preservation could enable us to conquer.*

Andreas Hansen described this same, horrifically transgressive moment of cannibalism:

It was a scene so ghastly that it will forever remain stamped upon my memory. We had been drinking salt water since Tuesday morning, but it did no good. Wednesday morning when I awoke, I was so thirsty and hungry that I was weak and dizzy. We drank salt water, but the more we drank the more we wanted, and so great was our thirst and so growing our hunger that we were driven to cut open the body of our dead companion. We had removed all his clothing and divided it between us. I cut open his stomach in the hope of finding water. At noon, I used my knife again. The pilot [Bertrand] *asked me for a piece of the flesh. I cut him a piece and gave it to him. My brain began to reel, and I knew nothing more.*

As the cruelly cold sun shone down on Marshall Bertrand, Andreas Hansen and the naked and partially cannibalized corpse of Alfred Swanson, it is difficult to imagine the horror they were in. Neither Bertrand nor Hansen ever confessed exactly how much human flesh and blood they reluctantly consumed to stay alive. As Wednesday moved on, they also observed sharks circling the small skiff they inhabited, their sharp fins and tails poking through the water, reminding the men of the inevitable and grisly death that surely awaited them both.

Bertrand and Hansen were lying almost in a stupor in the face of the winter sun, when suddenly, an image that may have been a mirage from their deepest dreams appeared before them. They both saw a ship outlined by the sun, perhaps a mile away and heading straight toward them. It couldn't be real—it must be madness. But Marshall Bertrand was willing to believe. He tore off his oilskin, leaving himself nearly as naked as the mutilated corpse at his feet. He then waved the oilskin above his head and screamed: "HELP! HELP! HELP US! PLEASE HELP US!"

Bertrand later said:

Just at this moment fortune aided me, our boat mounting high upon the crest of a long roller, so that it was thrown into full view of the lookout on the forecastle of the vessel. For a moment she held her course, and I feared that in the fading light we were not seen. A moment more and we knew better, for she came around before the wind…and she was headed straight toward us.

The ship *Emma F. Engel* was to be their salvation. Once Marshall Bertrand and Andreas Hansen were certain that they were about to be rescued, just before the *Engel* reached them, they both took the body of Alfred Swanson and threw it overboard, into the sea. Almost immediately, the sharks, "about

A modern version of a skiff, featuring a motor. *Photograph by Bradley Grillo, Wikimedia Commons.*

ten feet long," that had been circling their small skiff for hours consumed it, and the water around them turned red with blood. When asked later by a reporter from the *New York Times* why they had disposed of Swanson's corpse in this way, Hansen answered: "Why, it was so carved and mangled, and being naked, it was not fit for human eyes to rest upon. Oh, that was the last I ever saw of poor Al [Swanson]."

By 6:00 p.m. on Wednesday evening, both Marshall Bertrand and Andreas Hansen were resting comfortably in cabins below deck on the *Emma F. Engel*. The *New York Times* wrote that "for sixty hours they had nothing but salt water and the flesh and blood of their shipmate." At the time Hansen gave his account of events to reporters, it was said that Bertrand was in a deep sleep, unable to be awakened. I wonder what he dreamed about that night.

Forty-eight hours lost on the sea without food, water or adequate shelter—that is all it took for three men who knew one another so well to go insane, for one of them to declare they would murder another to drink their blood. Only a few more hours passed before the two surviving men stripped their dead friend's body naked, drank his blood and carved out and ate his flesh over and over again, all in the name of simple human survival. Two and a half days, sixty hours—that's all it took for Marshall Bertrand and Andreas Hansen to become cannibals.

The Irwin Lighthouse, Storm Raging, an 1851 painting of the Enoch Turley by James Wilson Carmichael. *Public domain.*

Think about their story and Alfred Swanson the next time you venture out into the ocean on a boat. The sea is a beautiful place that can bring you peace. But never forget that you are at its mercy. If you found yourself lost, far away from the shore in a small vessel with a few friends and almost no hope of rescue, ask yourself now: What would you do to survive?

Marshall Bertrand and Andreas Hansen faced no legal repercussions for their actions regarding the death and subsequent cannibalism of Alfred Swanson during their sixty hours of terror on the sea. After these horrific events, Hansen vanished from recorded history. But Marshall Bertrand continued in his sailor's life for forty more years until his death, although he never again spoke of the agony he endured during November 1884.

The *Enoch Turley,* the ship that Bertrand, Hansen and Swanson had come from, was lost at sea on April 6, 1889. It's said that on stormy, springtime nights, you can glimpse the phantom vessel on the Atlantic Ocean as one of the many ghost ships that haunts the Delaware coast.

4

ALIEN ENCOUNTERS IN THE FIRST STATE

One of the wonderful things about living in Delaware, especially in the rural parts of Sussex County, is stepping outside on a cloudless night and turning your eyes to the sky. Far away from the interference of city lights, the stars shine clearly in the darkness, making constellations easy to find. And as you watch the sky, you might see something strange, something that can't be an airplane because it's moving far too fast, its lights rapidly changing colors. Then you may realize that whatever this mysterious thing is, it is coming closer and closer to you. Its light may get brighter and brighter until it becomes blinding. You might be afraid; you can't move or scream.

And then suddenly, it's gone, and everything is normal again. The stars look the same as they did before, and the night is quiet, except for the soothing sounds of animals and insects in the woods nearby. Breathing a sigh of relief, you may laugh to yourself and go back inside the house. That's when you notice the time. It's somehow been four hours since you went outside to look at the stars, even though you swear you weren't out there for more than half an hour. Then you start to wonder: Did I just see a UFO? And then: Was I abducted by aliens from another world? You try to put it out of your mind. You decide not to tell a soul. Who would believe you anyway?

It might surprise you, but people have been seeing strange things in the sky for thousands of years. There are reports of unidentified flying objects and other phenomena dating to antiquity. Ancient cave paintings and artwork in Egyptian temples depict vessels coming from the heavens and odd-looking beings coming down to visit humans. One of the earliest written recordings of such an incident dates to 1440 BCE, when the scribes of Pharaoh

Thutmose III wrote of "flying disks" floating in the sky. In 218 BCE, the Roman historian Titus Livius, known as Livy, recorded that "phantom ships had been seen gleaming in the sky."

Delaware also has its own tales of unearthly things glimpsed in the heavens. There is an extraordinary article that was printed in the October 6, 1881 edition of the *Morning News* that was based in the city of Wilmington. Fifty-seven years before Orson Welles terrified the nation with his 1938 Halloween radio broadcast, *The War of the Worlds* (which many listeners believed was real), and sixty-six years before the 1947 Roswell incident made the possibility of aliens from other planets and galaxies visiting Earth an indelible part of our collective memory, this curious newspaper article appeared. This is a tale from over 140 years ago, in which many people over a vast amount of land all witnessed the same uncanny images in the sky. The following is the testimony from that weird and wondrous 1881 incident, as reported by the *Morning News.*

Peninsula people have been seeing ghosts and supernatural objects with alarming frequency during the last three weeks.…It is of some consolation to know, however, that if any people are deserving of a look ahead, behind the curtain and into the great unknown, it is the people of Delaware and the Eastern Shore.…As usual, it is not the rich man, but the poor man and his children who have seen these supernatural images and ghost-like goblins in the air.…

In Sussex County, Delaware, Monday night, two weeks ago, William West, a farmer living near Georgetown, the county seat, saw after nightfall, before the moon was fairly up above the horizon, whole platoons of angels marching in the clouds…bands of soldiers of great size, equipped with dazzling uniforms, their musket steels quivering and shimmering in the pale weird light that seemed to be everywhere.…The vision of startling distinctness had lasted long enough to be seen by a number of West's neighbors, who, after the unearthly military had taken its departure and been swallowed up in thin air, regaled the strange story to their eager friends.

An account of the occurrence appeared the next week in the Georgetown Inquirer. *But strangest of all, a man named Coverdale, who was driving through the country along a lonely road, at the same time, being several miles away from West's house, and in an entirely different direction, saw to his astonishment and alarm, the same band of soldiers in the sky. Many people living near Laurel, many miles away, situated at the lower end of the Peninsula, saw the same extraordinary phenomena at the same time.*

"Whole platoons of angels marching in the clouds."

The more the matter is looked into, the more unfathomable it gets. There has thus far been no satisfactory solution given to the series of mysterious specters in the sky.

For fifty years since its establishment in 1974, the National UFO Reporting Center (nuforc.org) has had the mission "to receive, record, and to the greatest degree possible, corroborate and document reports from individuals who have been witness to unusual, possibly UFO-related events." Overall, the center has received, to date, 170,000 first-person accounts, all of which are available to read online and many of which are accompanied by photographs. Out of all the states, Delaware ranks forty-eighth in terms of the number of reported UFO sightings. It is the second-smallest state, after all. However, as of this writing, the records of the NUFORC show over four hundred entries from Delaware dating from 1949 to the present day, with unexplained and eerie things witnessed by locals in literally every corner of the state. The following are a few of these recorded encounters with the otherworldly in the words of the people who experienced them.

The following account occurred in June 1954 in Claymont:

It was just before noon on a warm sunny June day. I was sixteen years old. Riding in the car with my brother-in-law driving, my sister riding in the front passenger seat, I was sitting in the back of a 1948 Plymouth. We were heading to a wedding breakfast at a place called Naaman's Teahouse on the corner of Naaman's Road and Philadelphia Pike. As we turned onto the driveway of the Teahouse and parked, I got out of the car (it was a four-door). I stood up and was facing toward the Delaware River. I barely had time to say "Look!" to my brother-in-law. And out of a bright white cloud came this huge almost silver disk-shaped object. It was headed toward our direction maybe about 600 feet in the air. From our vantage point it traveled about maybe two miles toward a stand of trees. No sooner had we saw it, it became ghostlike, as it headed toward a bank of puffy white clouds and became invisible again. This of course was before Star Trek *and how they used a cloaking device. If it was possible to have seen this craft up close, it would have been at least 300 feet in diameter. I said to my brother-in-law, "Did you see that?" He said, "Yeah!" I said, "Do we report it?" He said, "Nah, no one would believe us anyway." That was nearly fifty years ago, and I have never forgotten that incident or how the UFO looked. I'm 66 years old now and live about two miles from the Naaman's Teahouse and will always visualize that craft when I pass by.*

In May 1972, another witness had an encounter in Wilmington:

I was traveling up to Concord Mall on Route 202 with two friends. We took the scenic route. I was seventeen at the time. I remember we went around the last bend on 92 just before you get to Route 202 and all these cars were just stopped along the curve, in their tracks. We stopped too. We got out of the car and looked up to see this GIGANTIC glowing object, just about where the mall would be, hovering over that spot. It looked like a huge cylinder, with a cone-shaped end. It was glowing bright and incandescent. There seemed to be an electric humming sound, very faint. That is all I remember. We didn't remember going to the mall. I don't remember talking to the other people who were stopped. I only remember driving home with my friends in silence. There seems to be a huge chunk of missing time during and after the event. I don't remember ever talking about it after that, except years later I did call one of the friends to ask if she remembered it. She did.

In June 1984 in Seaford, two men experienced a possible alien abduction:

Me and a friend were night fishing in a pond in Seaford. First, we heard a sound coming from somewhere on the other side of the trees like a winding noise, loud. Then a few minutes after it stopped, a red glowing light appeared in the middle of the tree line. It started circling the pond up and down while still in the tree line, silent. I can't recall anything after that.

In June 1985 in Wilmington, two young girls encountered something that terrified them, a thing that did not seem human:

My friend and I, 13 and 15 years old, were walking to her paper route. It was light but not fully. I lived on an industrial street, no businesses were open, so no one was expected to be around at that time of day. At 5:30–6:00 a.m., a tall, white, thin, partially solid/translucent-like figure walked from behind a building. It was about thirty feet away. I froze as soon as I saw it. It took a few steps then stopped, turned its head, and looked at us. I thought I was going to die, I was so scared, worried I was seeing something I was not supposed to see. The figure looked at us for several seconds then started to walk again. It went up a small embankment towards a creek. We ran, did the paper route, then later, when we told the story, no one believed us.

The presence of Dover Air Force Base may partially account for the state's low number of reported UFO sightings. Residents who live nearby are used to seemingly unusual aircraft in their midst. However, this account from September 1990 just south of Dover stands out:

We were camping at a private campground when we heard a very strange sound and looked up to see what at first appeared to be a jet airplane passing by the campsite very slowly and at a very low altitude, as if it were landing. The sound was very foreign and did not sound like any aircraft either of us had ever heard. Then the craft became silent and seemed to disappear over some trees. We then went out to a nearby field to see if we could figure out what it could have been and where it went. We saw nothing for a long while. As we decided to go back to our campsite, I noticed what appeared to be a falling star. I pointed out the location where I saw the light drop, when, all of a sudden, a craft slowly approached us. It was triangular in shape and huge as it came to a stop right in front of us, almost above us. We noticed that it made no sound whatsoever. My friend noted that it did not have any flashing red light that all registered aircraft are required to display. Right after he stated that, a large red light began to glow at the bottom, center of the craft. As soon as that

"I was seeing something I was not supposed to see."

occurred, we freaked out, thinking that the occupants of the craft may have somehow heard us and responded. We then witnessed as the craft swiftly drifted away silently then sped upward at what appeared to be a 45 degree angle until it went out of sight.

While driving cars, people often report unusual interference with electronics when UFOs are near, like this account that occurred in Lewes, Delaware, on November 29, 2005:

I was driving home from work as usual when the radio station changed. I changed the station back, but it changed again. I decided to turn off the radio, and as I reached for it, I saw a brilliant white light out of the corner of my eye. I looked over in shock and saw six streams of light, shooting around my car. I promptly sped up and they flew ahead of me. Once they were out of sight, the radio came back on by itself.

If you find yourself driving through Milton, Delaware, you might suddenly screech to a halt as you reach the Eagle Crest Aerodrome, a private airport established in 1952, and see what appears to be a flying saucer from Mars on the ground nearby. It is one of the First State's most famous curiosities, and seldom does a week go by without folks stepping out of their vehicles to take a photograph of it. What you're looking at is a Futuro House. Only ninety-six of them were made, and two of them found a home in Delaware—and are still standing. One is in the town of Houston, but the Futuro House in Milton has become a quintessential roadside attraction.

The spaceship-like dwellings were the brainchild of Finnish architect Matti Suuronen, who was asked by a friend to build a "ski-cabin" that could heat up quickly. Suuronen designed a home in the spirit of an RV whose exterior was made of fiberglass-reinforced plastic, an innovation at the time. In his book *You Wouldn't Believe: 44 Strange and Wondrous Delmarva Tales*, author Jim Duffy describes the unique virtues of a Futuro home:

The cabin was elevated on four legs, each bolted to its own concrete "pier"—those piers were much easier to lay than a full foundation. Thanks to the then-latest innovations in polyurethane insulation, the interior could heat up from minus 20 degrees Fahrenheit to a comfy 60 degrees in just 30 minutes. The cabin stands 13 feet off the ground. Its entrance would have seemed like magic in an old sci-fi movie, but it works basically like a modern garage door opener: Push the button on a remote, and a stairway

"A craft slowly approached us."

descends to the ground. The saucer you then climb up into has a diameter of 26 feet. Squeezed inside: a bedroom, bathroom, kitchen, and dining room. Later on, some models would offer a fireplace option.

In the 1960s and 1970s, when American popular culture was obsessed with aliens and the limitless possibilities of what the future could bring, the Futuro House seemed like a safe bet. You could comfortably live in your own flying saucer for just $16,000. An enterprising man named Joe Hudson began to open showings of Futuro Houses in southern Delaware, and he said, "We had long lines of people wanting to see inside, especially on weekends. Sometimes, it was so crowded inside that people couldn't move. We had a lot of orders."

Top: Finnish architect Matti Suuronen, the creator of the Futuro. *Wikimedia Commons.*

Bottom: A Futuro house. *Photograph by J-P Karna, Wikimedia Commons.*

Sadly, in the 1970s, plastic, the primary material in the external construction of the Futuro Homes, became much more expensive. Also, Delaware politicians, including the mayor of Lewes, spoke publicly against the addition of flying saucer–like dwellings in their community. But still, two of the Futuro Houses still survive in Delaware. The one in Milton was originally used as an office for the staff of the Eagle Crest Aerodrome, but it had subsequently been rented for many years by a man named Rich Garrett, who said he has loved living in this unusual space. A 2016 article written by James Fisher and Jason N. Minto for the *News Journal* says:

> *From the outside, the home has a UFO's silhouette, looking like a sphere evenly flattened to a doughnut's shape....On the inside, as Garrett pointed out in a tour, nearly every furnishing and trim piece is shallowly curved, since the home itself has no right-angle walls. Countertops, closet doors, seats: all sloped.*

Living inside a UFO has its small drawbacks, according to Rich Garrett. There's no real closet space, so "one tends not to acquire so much." But the rent can't be beat. And the keys Garrett received from his landlord came with a simple handwritten label with two words: "SPACE SHIP."

5
The Lonely Lady of the Dunes

For Brandi

Having a loved one who works on the ocean can be a fearful thing, especially centuries ago, when sailors could be on the high seas for years at a time with no way to contact the people who were waiting for them back at home. In the old days, you kissed your sweetheart goodbye as they ascended the deck of the mighty ship that would become their whole world and waved as the vessel sailed into the horizon. You could do nothing but hope and pray your beloved would return to you safely, that no storms or pirates would bring them harm. Months or years would pass, and then one day, your lover, your sibling or your child would return home to you. Those were the good times. But sometimes, they just never came back.

The 1938 book *Delaware: A Guide to the First State*, compiled by the Federal Writers' Project, relates the story of "the sailor's ghost." In the city of Wilmington on French Street, there was a house with a well in its backyard. As the tale goes, in 1783, a sailor named French Kellum and his wife rented a room in this house from a landlady. They had not lived there long when it came time for Kellum to go out to sea again. He bid his wife goodbye and sailed on a ship bound for the West Indies. Months went by with no word from the vessel. It never reached its intended destination. Finally, French Kellum's wife accepted that her husband and the ship had fallen victim to the sea, leaving her a widow.

One dark and stormy night, the widow and the landlady were awoken by terrifying moans and screams that seemed to be coming from behind

"The wife fainted dead away."

the house. Dressed in their nightgowns and carrying flickering candles, they listened as the unearthly sounds echoed even louder than nature's thunder. Then as suddenly as they had begun, the nightmarish wailing ceased. The wife and the landlady had almost finished breathing a sigh of relief when there came three sharp knocks on the back door. Slowly, very slowly, the wife and landlady crept toward the door and opened it. And there stood the ghost of French Kellum covered in mud, his face dripping with seawater. He had risen from his watery grave to see his wife one last time. The wife fainted at the horrifying sight and, for a time, knew nothing more.

When she again regained consciousness, the face of her husband was the first thing she saw. She screamed, but then she soon realized that things were not as they appeared to be. Her husband was not a ghost; he was quite alive. French Kellum explained that his ship had finally made it back to Wilmington the previous night, and he walked home as the great thunderstorm began. Along the way, he slipped and fell in some mud. Once home, he decided to wash up using water from the well before going into the house. Unfortunately, he then had the bad luck of falling into the well, and its heavy lid dropped shut. The moaning and screaming that the women had heard came from him trying to get out of the well, which he finally did, and then he knocked at the door. Hearing this explanation, the wife of French Kellum laughed with joy as she realized she truly had her husband back, safe by her side. He was alive, not a sea-soaked ghost.

That's a story in which a loved one returning from the sea ended happily, where the ghost is not truly a ghost at all. But there is another story I want to tell you, one that ends in tragedy and creates a specter that has been seen by countless witnesses over the past several hundred years.

———◆———

DELAWARE'S SEASHORE STATE PARK is one of the state's treasures, offering visitors a plethora of activities to enjoy in the splendor of the great outdoors. You can sunbathe on the sand or swim and surf in the ocean. You can fish, walk through a nature trail and have a picnic, rent a boat from the marina and go sailing, and there are several campsites throughout the park for those who want to stay overnight.

If you have ever gone to any of the First State's beaches, you drove past Seashore State Park as you crossed the Indian River Inlet Bridge, a bridge that some whisper is cursed. The bridge that you cross today is the fifth

Indian River Inlet Bridge in Delaware Seashore State Park. *Photograph by Antony-22, Wikimedia Commons.*

constructed over the inlet that connects the Indian River Bay with the Atlantic Ocean. The first was built using wood in 1934, and due to the maritime conditions, it quickly deteriorated and became unsafe. Just four years later, in 1938, construction on the second bridge began. This time, the bridge was made of steel and concrete. It opened in 1940, but just eight years later, a tragedy occurred. The winter of 1948 was a harsh one in Delaware. The tide was unusually high, and the winter wind howled ferociously. Thick coatings of ice scoured deep marks into the piers that supported the bridge, and all these elements together caused the bridge to collapse on February 10, 1948. At the time of the disaster, a pickup truck was on the bridge. The three men inside the truck were plunged into the icy water and drowned.

The third bridge was completed in 1952 but lasted only a decade. It was closed after being severely damaged in the notorious Ash Wednesday storm of 1962, one of the most destructive storms to ever hit the Atlantic coast. The fourth bridge opened in 1965 and added a second span in 1976. But again, by 1986, it became clear the bridge was becoming unsafe. Temporary measures secured the short-term safety of the bridge, but in 1999, it was stated that only one more bad storm could cause the bridge to collapse. Given that, on average, twenty-eight thousand vehicles crossed the bridge

Indian River Life Saving Station. *Photograph by Smallbones, Wikimedia Commons.*

during the summer months, there was a possibility of catastrophic loss of human life. The fifth and current bridge was opened to traffic in 2012. Since its creation, there have been reports from drivers who witnessed an old-fashioned pickup truck driving in front of them that mysteriously vanishes, perhaps a ghostly reenactment of the tragedy of 1948.

Part of Delaware's Seashore State Park, the Indian River Life-Saving Station, is designated as a National Historic Site. The Victorian architecture is impossible to miss, and today, it is a museum that should be visited. As shipwrecks along the Delaware coast were common, the Indian River Life-Saving Station was opened in 1876. Ed Okonowicz, in his book *Terrifying Tales 2 of the Beaches and the Bays*, describes the building's history and purpose:

> *For 86 years, the station keeper and his crew of six or seven surfmen worked year round under hazardous conditions. Each night, in fair weather and foul, they regularly walked the beaches, searching the coastline for a craft that might be in trouble. During storms, the surfmen were called upon to do a bit more, namely, to conduct daring sea rescues in harrowing gales, ice storms, and even life-threatening hurricanes. These rescue operations were extremely dangerous. Interpreters at the present-day museum tell visitors*

that, when referring to the surfmen's duty to try and save those in trouble at sea, the lifesaving services motto was: "You have to go out, but you don't have to come back." Along the treacherous Delaware coastline, the site of hundreds of shipwrecks and an untold number of deaths, fishermen and locals first reported sightings of a ghost as early as the 1890s.

According to Ed Okonowicz and the legends that have been handed down throughout the generations in Delaware, the name of this ghost is Molly McGwinn, and this is her story.

———•———

In the old days, when pirates like Captain Kidd and Blackbeard (both of whom are said to have buried treasure in Delaware that people are still searching for, and the community of Blackbird is named after the latter) sailed the Atlantic, shipwrecks along the coast of Delaware were routine. And the likelihood that those ships carried a fortune in gold and silver was enticing. To this day, there is a section of the First State's coast known as "Coin Beach," where you can regularly see people with metal detectors hoping to find the motherlode.

Ed Okonowicz wrote of the scavenging of an earlier time that gave birth to a haunting:

When ships crashed upon rocks, damaged cargo and dead passengers were delivered onto the beaches. Often, during the height of the storm—and to be sure, within a short time after its end—bands of locals would swoop down from the dunes and race each other to claim the pickings. These sea scavengers would strip the clothes off dead bodies, pull jewels from bloated fingers and pry gold from the teeth of the recently departed. They reasoned that it was their right to put their loot to good use, for the coin and clothing and precious stones were of no use to the dead, nor was the cargo of building materials, spices, food, livestock, or furniture. With regularity, when the weather and sea created a storm that delivered an unexpected prize to the shoreline, the body pickers were ready to go to work and claim all they could carry.

But when Mother Nature did not supply a storm to wreck a ship, it became necessary to create the circumstances in which a wreck could occur and provide a livelihood for the unsavory creatures who feasted on human

"Pirates such as Captain Kidd and Blackbeard sailed the seas."

disaster. That is where Molly McGwinn comes into this tale. Folklore says that Molly emigrated from Ireland to the United States, eventually becoming an indentured servant to a family of sea wreck scavengers based in what is now known as the town of Ocean View. Molly was not one of the pickers; hers was a different and more important job. During the times when the weather was clear, it was Molly's charge to stand on top of the highest dune of the Delaware coast with a lantern in her hand. Her purpose was to make incoming ships think her light was that of a lighthouse, and instead of finding protection, the vessels tempted by her light would crash on the unforgiving rocks—all the better for the picking.

Could you have done what Molly did? Imagine standing on the top of a sandy dune, holding a heavy lantern as high as you can raise it. Imagine watching a ship come nearer and nearer to the shore, the souls aboard it thinking they were safe. Then imagine the awful sound of the ship's timbers splintering as it hits the rocks. Imagine hearing the screams of the men, women and children aboard that ship as they suddenly realized they were going to a watery grave. And afterward, imagine the terrible silence as their drowned bodies, along with the ship's treasure, washed up on the shore. It would then be your task to shine your lantern over the corpses as the pickers did their despicable work. Could you do it?

"Could you have done what Molly did?"

Molly hated what she had to do, but she felt she had no choice. She longed to leave and go back home to Ireland—if a way of escaping could be found. At last, Molly fell in love with a sailor named Nathan. He promised to carry Molly away from all this as soon as he made one final voyage out to sea to make his fortune. For six months, Molly waited for Nathan to return to the coast of Delaware. In the meantime, she continued to hold her lantern on top of the dunes, a siren who would be fatal to any ship that answered her call.

One moonlit night, Molly did her hateful work as usual, watching and listening as a great ship and all the souls on board succumbed to the rocks and the waves. Again, Molly made her descent to the beach with her lantern to give light to the heartless scavengers who preyed on the dead. But this night, this terrible night, was different than the others. As Molly showed the lantern light on the poor victims of this wreck, she saw the face of her beloved Nathan. He had indeed finally returned to her—but not in the way she had dreamed of. The pickers were puzzled as Molly let out an anguished scream to the night sky, and then she bent down to kiss the cold, dead lips of Nathan, her lover, her final chance of a new life ruined forever by her own hand.

The pickers let out a cry of annoyance as Molly flung her lantern down to the sand, taking away their light. And then they watched as Molly McGwinn walked straight into the sea, welcoming the final, fatal embrace of the ocean's waves, determined to meet her beloved Nathan in heaven. But that is not what seems to have happened. Ever since that fateful night, the lonely ghost of Molly has been seen by many witnesses, and her tragic story has been told around countless campfires by those who dare to stay at Delaware Seashore State Park at night. Her restless spirit is known by many names: the Ghost Girl, Shipwreck Molly, the Dune Demon.

One of the most frightening sightings of Molly's restless spirit was reported to authors Charles Adams III and David Seibold, and they recorded it in their wonderful book *Ghost Stories of the Delaware Coast*. They interviewed a couple who wished to remain anonymous, and they related an unforgettable encounter they had as they walked on the beach near the Indian River Life-Saving Station:

> *I guess it was around ten o'clock that night.…I almost hate to say this, but I really do believe it was a full moon that night, or at least very close to it.…On the horizon of the ocean, we saw some ships or boats. Way, way up ahead, we saw some people walking north. We remarked to each*

Delaware Seashore State Park. *Photograph by Acroterion, Wikimedia Commons.*

other how amazing it was that we seemed to have the beach all to ourselves. Along this one stretch were some pretty high dunes. Now, we had been looking up and down the beach and like I said, we were almost alone except for those other people way ahead of us. Well, all of a sudden, as if she just popped up out of nowhere, just a few yards ahead of us, was a young girl. It was weird right from the start….There seemed to be no way we could have missed seeing her as we looked up ahead. But she appeared as if out of nowhere. Well, we just walked along, ready to nod hello to the girl as we passed her. But then, something even stranger happened….All of a sudden, just off to our right, I heard, you know, violent sound coming from the water. There was thumping, splashing, and even a whining and moaning sound….Sure enough, there was one small area of the beach and surf which was being churned up…splashing and thrashing and it looked like there was nothing causing it.

Nothing spooky with us until, sort of instinctively, we looked back to our left and to where the girl had been. She was still there. But instead of sitting on the edge of a dune like she was when we first saw her… she was standing up. I couldn't believe my eyes. I was scared too much to even move….Then we heard it. The girl started to talk. It was a low, very quiet: "Help…help me…please help me." You could barely hear it over the natural sound of the ocean….And as time went on, she seemed to fade and fade a little more. I don't think she walked toward us, but I know it looked like she was going to. But just about at the time she might have, she started to disappear.

If you ever find yourself on a Delaware beach at twilight, enamored of the peace and relaxation offered by walking along the sand and the waves, think of Molly. And if, after the sun sets, you see a lantern's light mysteriously appear at the top of the nearest dune, it may be time for you to go home. If you don't, the lonely lady, the tragic spirit of Molly McGwinn, may decide she wants to meet you and take you with her into the depths of the sea. Tell her legend to your friends around the fire as you camp at Delaware Seashore State Park and see what happens after you extinguish all your lights and try to go to sleep.

Go on, I dare you.

6

APPARITIONS IN OLD NEW CASTLE

Founded in 1640, only nine years after the founding of the town of Lewes in present-day Sussex County, New Castle is one of the oldest and the most well-preserved towns in the state of Delaware. Its historic district consists of nearly five hundred structures, and if your imagination can block out the cars and contemporary traffic lights, it is very easy to walk around New Castle and feel that you are in the seventeenth or eighteenth century. Also like Lewes, New Castle is one of the most haunted towns in the First State, and it may even justly take the prize for being the most haunted of all. On its 135 acres of land, there are multitudes of ghosts from the past that continue to make their presence known to those living in the twenty-first century.

The area now known as New Castle was originally called Tomakonck, which means "place of the beaver." The Dutch were the first Europeans to colonize the area, but it was seized by the Swedes in 1654. In an astonishing turn of events, the Dutch reclaimed the colony only a year later, giving it the name of New Amstel, after the Amstel River located in Holland. The Dutch created a grid pattern of streets as their settlement grew larger, and they established a town square, or "green," that still exists today. However, just nine years later, the area was seized by the English, who changed the name of the town to New Castle and made it the capital of the Delaware Colony. In 1680, New Castle was part of the lands "given" to William Penn, and it was here that Penn first set foot on North American soil, arriving on October 27, 1682. Today, a statue of William Penn on the town green commemorates this consequential moment in history.

The Green in New Castle. *Photograph by Ataraxy22, Wikimedia Commons.*

In 1934, the New Castle Historical Society (NCHS) was founded by a group of citizens to save and preserve one of the town's most historic buildings (the Amstel House, which you will hear more about soon). Today, the society's mission is to "collect, preserve, and promote awareness of New Castle history to its members, citizens, and visitors, and to support the preservation of historical resources. To this end, the society preserves and interprets the Amstel and Dutch Houses, the Old Library, and The Arsenal, is active in the study of local history, and disseminates valued historical information and stories through exhibits, events, programs, publications, and resource material." Unlike many historical societies, the NCHS does not shy away from speaking about the ghostly or macabre aspects of the town's past. On the contrary, it embraces it, believing as I do that telling these stories can be a gateway to further learning. For about twenty-five years and counting, the NCHS has offered its outstanding Hauntings in History tours to sold-out crowds during weekend evenings leading up to Halloween in October.

Michael Connelly, who has been associated with the NCHS for twelve years as of this writing and currently serves as its executive director, was kind enough to grant me an interview, in which he shared his thoughts about New Castle's rich history, its ghost stories and a few of his own personal experiences. "It's an incredibly well-preserved community," Connelly said.

It's really kind of a microcosm of American history, from the very earliest settlements in the seventeenth century all the way up to current times. It includes everything: from stories about the Colonial period to the Revolution, to struggles with slavery and war, to changes in transportation and industry. It really is just sort of a small, little town where you can easily talk about anything in American history and have a local connection to it. And you can do that with most towns, I think, but this one spans 375 years, so it really does cover it all.

The NCHS moved into its current building, which has a haunted history of its own, in 2015. Michael Connelly told me,

This building used to be a federal arsenal. It was barracks for some troops from Fort Delaware. It was a quarantine hospital for a cholera epidemic. It's been a bunch of things. So, the story associated with this building when it [was also previously] *a restaurant, people in the restaurant used to think there was the ghost of an old nurse who was here, I guess from the cholera outbreak. They nicknamed her Rosie, and she was said to disrupt table settings and turn the water on and off in the bathrooms, make an appearance in the bathroom apparently. Since we've been here, we've continued to hear some weird things in the bathrooms with water being turned on, or running when it wasn't supposed to be running—when nobody else was around. The hand dryers going on and off, they do that*

The historic sheriff's house and jail. *Photograph by Ataraxy22, Wikimedia Commons.*

quite a bit. And then we have a story of one of our staff members whose keys were misplaced—she couldn't find them. She went searching all over the place for them, and after quite a while of searching, she ended up back at her desk where she had started looking for them and found the keys. They were in her trashcan. But they were underneath the trashcan liner, below the bag. So, she's like, "How'd they get here?" She's the last person in the building at the time, so she got the heck out of here really quickly! I don't know what it is, but these things keep happening.

Connelly also shared with me some of the information the NCHS has gathered over the years about several of the town's most haunted locations. Let's take a tour to visit some of the many apparitions of Olde New Castle.

THE DAVID FINNEY INN

The David Finney Inn is perhaps one of the most haunted buildings in the city. There are many ghost stories that center on this building:

There seems to be some type of unknown presence on the third floor of the building. When the inn was for sale several years ago, the owner at the time was showing a realtor around the building. She had a little dog with her. That dog followed her everywhere, always right at her heels. But when they started to go up the stairs to the third floor, the dog stopped at the bottom of the stairs and refused to follow them up. At another time, when the building was being renovated following a fire, the owner always left his two Dobermans in the building overnight for security. He said that they, too, would never follow him up to the third floor.

A previous owner investigated the third floor following several complaints by overnight guests that the windows in their rooms would not stay closed. One night, when no one was staying at the inn, he decided to experiment by closing all the windows and placing sticks diagonally between the top sash and the corner of the window so it couldn't open accidentally. He locked the doors and spent the night on the third floor to make sure no one entered the rooms. The next morning, when he unlocked the rooms, all the windows were wide open, and the sticks were placed neatly on the dresser across the room.

Employees of the inn have told many stories. Once of the bartenders told us about an early morning, where she and another waiter and waitress were opening the building. There was no one else there. She was standing behind the bar, and the others were sitting on barstools across from her. Suddenly, she saw her coworker throw her head back like she was falling or was pushed. When the bartender stopped to ask her friend if she was okay, she was suddenly pushed backward. The other waiter witnessed the whole event. They didn't see anyone. When I asked the bartender if she was afraid, she said she wasn't; she felt that it was more like a practical joke.

She did have another incident that did frighten her. She was closing that time. She was alone on the second floor and went to close and lock the office. The hallway was completely dark. All of a sudden, she heard a small voice call her name. She thought it was her imagination or a door squeaking, so she ignored it. She heard the sound again, and this time it was very clearly calling her name. She said she was so scared she ran down the front steps. When she got to the bar, there were only a few people in the building. They all claimed that they had been busy on the first floor and that no one had gone upstairs or had called her name.

THE AMSTEL HOUSE

The Amstel House, now a museum operated by the New Castle Historical Society, was New Castle's first grand mansion when it was built in 1738. It is also one of the most haunted locations in the city. There are many legends and stories related to the house—some true and some not true. One of the most lingering false stories is that the Amstel House is connected by a tunnel to the David Finney Inn, allowing the same ghost to haunt both locations. While some eighteenth-century buildings do have tunnels, usually for ventilation purposes, there is no evidence of a tunnel ever existing in or at the Amstel House.

The most notable ghost story related to the Amstel House is that of an apparition that has come to be known as "The Lady in Blue." The apparition has been said to appear in the upstairs windows of the house and was noticed by passersby on the street below. Her name refers to the blue dress or gown that she is wearing when she appears. No one knows the identity of the Lady in Blue. Reports of her appearances have largely ceased

The Amstel House. *Photograph by Pubdog, Wikimedia Commons.*

since the Historical Society installed blinds on the windows to keep sunlight out of the museum. Nonetheless, inside the house, the staff and volunteers still report occasional strange experiences and noises in the building.

In the 1940s, a live-in curator at the museum, Mrs. Dundas, used to report that she heard "her" footsteps moving up and down the staircase and through the halls of the house. One night, Mrs. Dundas reports very heavy footsteps on the stairs outside her bedroom. They did not sound like the footsteps she had grown accustomed to hearing. She became concerned, because there was a recent rash of burglaries plaguing the town. So, she believed the culprit may now be in her house. Mrs. Dundas was a formidable lady and decided to confront the burglar. She left her room and walked to the staircase landing. There, she saw a shadowy figure standing before her. She decided to push the fellow down the stairs. She stepped forward and pushed toward the figure, but her hands were met with only empty air. She then watched as the shadowy figure descended the stairs, disappearing into the parlor at the bottom.

More recently, a museum volunteer, while out for an early morning walk, reported hearing a woman singing inside the Amstel House. As she walked past the old kitchen window of the house, she distinctly heard someone inside singing. This surprised her since she did not expect anyone to be in the museum that early in the morning. She walked to the front door and knocked but received no answer. She continued to walk around the building to see if anyone was there or any doors were open. Nothing was amiss. By the time she returned to the kitchen window, the singing had stopped. When she asked the museum director if someone was in the building that morning, he said, "No." He was the first person to arrive at about 9:00 a.m., and she experienced the singing before 7:00 a.m. This is the first time anyone had ever reported hearing a woman's voice inside the house.

When I asked NCHS executive director Michael Connelly if he had ever experienced anything "odd" at any of the historic locations in town. He replied that he had experienced strange things at the Amstel House on more than one occasion:

One day, it was a Tuesday afternoon, and it was like one o'clock or two o'clock in the afternoon, and the only two people in the building were me and an intern from the University of Delaware. I was sitting at my desk; she was sitting at another one, just working along. It was a normal, sunny afternoon—no big deal. All of a sudden, we hear this big, like really loud, BANG that comes from downstairs. And I jumped up. I'm running. Because it's a museum, I'm expecting to find a giant portrait that has fallen off the wall or something like that. So, I run downstairs, and I'm looking through the first floor of the building, and I can't find anything that's wrong. So, I thought, "Well maybe it's one of our shutters," because we have real shutters on the building and they swing back and forth, but they're held in place normally. I went outside to look around, and there was nothing amiss anywhere. So, I came back up and said, "I don't know what it was." So, we really didn't think much more about it.

A week goes by, and she's back in; it's literally the same scenario: it's a nice day, I'm sitting there working, she's sitting there working. It's very close to the same time of day, and we hear the same noise, BANG, again. And we both looked at each other like, "You've got to be kidding me." So, I get up again and start making my way downstairs, and I'm about halfway down the staircase, and I hear it again—BANG—really loud. And this time, it sounds like it's coming from the old kitchen of the house, which is sort of in the back wing of the building. So, I go there first, and there's nothing wrong. I can't find anything out of place that would make that noise. I run the circuit through the building; I go outside, look at all the shutters, and there's nothing. I have no idea what it was. I think it's really weird that I heard the same noise a week apart and had the same experience, like "we can't figure out what it is." And after that, we never heard it again.

———◆———

THE TERRIBLE DEATH OF CATHERINE BEVAN

One of the most macabre tales from the history of New Castle and the First State as a whole is the story of Catherine Bevan, who was the first woman to be executed in the state of Delaware. She murdered her husband, Henry, with the help of her lover, Peter Murphy, on April 3, 1731. After being found guilty, she was put to death on the New Castle green on June 10, 1731. The following account comes directly from a newspaper article contemporary to Catherine's execution, the manner of which was her being publicly burned at the stake:

> *When Henry Bevan of New Castle, Delaware, "reckoned near 60 years of age," died unexpectedly, his neighbors were suspicious. They had suspected Henry's wife Catherine, "upwards of 50," of having too familiar an intimacy with a young servant of the household, one Peter Murphy. Henry himself had frequently complained to his neighbors that, "his Wife and Servant beat and abused him," and many felt that the old man may have had, "not fair usage."*
>
> *Rumor being rife in the area, a county Magistrate decided to attend the funeral and was shocked to find that, "the Coffin had been nailed up before any of the Company came." The Magistrate ordered the coffin to be pried open and thereupon found the corpse of Henry Bevan to be terribly bruised and other signs of violence apparent. A Coroner's Inquest was called and after they viewed, "those Bruises etc. that were visible in several Parts of his Body," the opinion was expressed that the unfortunate Henry Bevan had met his demise through violent means.*
>
> *Catherine Bevan and Peter Murphy were, "immediately committed [arrested] upon Suspicion." At first, they both protested their innocence and denied their guilt. Once they were separated, however, Peter Murphy could not withstand the pressure of interrogation and confessed. Murphy claimed, "That his Mistress sent him to New Castle to buy some Rat's Bane, or,*

New Castle Courthouse Museum. *Photograph by Ataraxy22, Wikimedia Commons.*

if he could not get that, some Roman Vitriol." Murphy couldn't find any Rat's Bane so he settled for the Vitriol which they, "gave her Husband to drink dissolved in a Glass of Wine," but the old man immediately vomited it up and fearing, "it would not have the desired effect," the pair decided on a more certain path.

Peter Murphy claimed that Catherine had him, "Beat his Master well, especially about the Breast, till he should grow so weak that she might be able to deal with him and leave the rest to her." Accordingly this was done until, "the old man could no longer stand." He then confessed that the pair moved Bevan to the couch where, "his Wife twisted a handkerchief around his Neck in order to strangle him." At this time Peter Murphy left for, "Former Neighbors who lived at a Distance," to inform them that Catherine Bevan's husband, "was in a Fit, and she feared he would die in it, and desired them to come to the House immediately." Peter testified that he returned to the Bevan household before the neighbor's arrival and found Henry Bevan dead, and that his Mistress informed him, "I have had two hard Struggles with the old Man since you went away, and he like to have been too strong for me both Times, but I have quieted him at last." So that was Peter Murphy's tale. Catherine Bevan denied it all. Peter Murphy repeated this tale at trial. The Court believed his testimony and both Peter and Catherine were found guilty of the murder of Henry Bevan.

The Court passed sentence that the man was to be hanged and the woman strangled and burned at the stake, burning being the penalty for a wife's murder of her sovereign lord. The punishment for a female petit treason *was predicated on the notion that such a punishment would spare a female's modesty as her corpse would be spared the ritual humiliation that often accompanied the punishment of the male.*

After sentence was passed Peter Murphy changed his tune. Before the scheduled execution Murphy declared Catherine innocent of the crimes he ascribed to her. He claimed to have, "wronged her much," that she did not tie the handkerchief round her Husband's Neck, and that the chief of his Evidence at Court was false; but that he was the Promoter of all that happened, and confessed to all that was done. Catherine continued to deny "to the last that she acted any Part in the Murder." The Court had no take with last minute confessions and the executions were carried out as scheduled on June 10, 1731. It was reported that, "Neither of them said much at the Place of Execution: The Man seems penitent, but the Woman appeared hardened."

It was custom when burning a free woman to place a cord around their neck and draw it tight as the flames were lit in an effort to mitigate the sufferings of one so penalized. In Catherine Bevan's case, when the fire was lit it broke out, "in a stream which pointed directly on the Rope that went Round her Neck, and burnt it off instantly, so that she fell into the Flames, and was seen to struggle" until she was dead.

The NCHS's research on the case of Catherine Bevan finishes this dark tale:

Some people say that on a cool, autumn night, when the wind is blowing and the leaves are rustling across the Green, you can still hear Catherine Bevan whispering, "I am innocent."

The Dutch House

The structure known as the Dutch House is one of the oldest still standing in the state of Delaware. It was constructed in the late seventeenth century, around 1680, and is now operated as a museum by the New Castle Historical

Society. The Dutch House was the only other location where current NCHS executive director Michael Connelly felt that he may have experienced the paranormal. He said near the end of our interview:

> *I don't know if this a real experience or not, but I'll tell you the story anyway. In our Dutch House museum, it's vacant every day until there's a tour. We don't have a staff person in the building normally, and that's the way it's been for many, many years. But I will go over there occasionally to do something—clean it up, set something up, or whatever. It used to be that when we had a landline phone in there, that phone would ring. And I'd pick it up, and there's be nobody on the line. It would just be dead air. The phone number wasn't a published number in the phonebook, so people wouldn't have any reason to call it normally. So, I just thought it was some weird thing happening with the phone and never really paid it much attention.*
>
> *Then one of our guides told me that she had an unusual tour one weekend. She said the people that came on tour, one of them was sensitive, or psychic, or something, to spirits. And she said the person, at the end of the tour, said, "That was a really great tour. I don't want you to think I'm weird, but I've gotta tell you something. When we first walked into that house," (when you walk into the Dutch House, you walk into a very small vestibule, and there's doorways to the right and left) she said, "When I walked into that vestibule, right to the left, I saw this shadowy figure standing there. I got the sense it wasn't anything bad, but this figure, entity, or whatever, had been trying to communicate with us. But it had been unable to reach us." I have no idea what that is, but I immediately made the connection: So, that's who's been calling me. Gotcha.*

I concluded my interview with NCHS executive director Michael Connelly by asking him why he and his colleagues, unlike workers in many other similar organizations, were not hesitant to embrace the darker and haunting aspects of New Castle's history in their programming. This was Mr. Connelly's answer:

> *I think it's just part of the general culture. A lot of communities—I think every community—has its ghost stories here and there. It's part of the folklore. It's the way people sort of entertain themselves. There is a way to combine it with history so people remember* more *of the history....I always said that when we did these public paranormal investigations, I would give them a five minute speech about who lived here and when and*

what they did, that kind of thing. And I always said that I guarantee you the people on the paranormal tours remember the names of the people that I just told them far better than any of our regular tourists. Because, for the next two and a half hours, they're going through the Amstel House asking for Nicholas Van Dyke and nobody remembers who Nicholas Van Dyke was, but if you're constantly trying to reach him and talk to him….So, I think there's some benefit to it. Everybody experiences historic sites in different ways. And historic sites, whether they be battlefields or buildings, houses, they can be powerful places where people can connect with the past. So, if that means they're connecting with that place because there's a ghost story associated with it, or they think they're experiencing something, or they are experiencing something—that's a different way. Who's to say that's any better or worse than somebody who's coming in to look at a Chippendale chair from 1770? It's just a different way people are going to experience the place. And this attracts audiences we wouldn't otherwise reach. It gets people into New Castle, introduces them to the history, so when they come on a ghost tour, they say, "Wow, this is awesome, what other stuff do you guys do here?" And they come back.

If you are interested in visiting one of the most historic and perhaps the most haunted town in the state of Delaware, New Castle cannot be missed. And you never know, in the process of looking for apparitions from the past, you might also learn other things you'll never forget.

7
SOME SKELETONS IN THE CLOSET

In one of Delaware's oldest towns, there is a house that has, for generations, been called the "Castle" by local residents. This grand old Victorian Gothic Revival mansion was designed by famed Baltimore architects Thomas and James Dixon in 1855. It contains over forty rooms and luxurious period furnishings, and it boasts a five-story-tall tower that looms over the community in which it stands. For many years in the latter part of the twentieth century, the Castle was operated as a bed-and-breakfast. Now, it is a private residence, which is why I am choosing to be secretive about its exact location. But this old house has a long history of being haunted, and the ghostly legends that have been whispered about it by those who have been brave enough to live within its walls deserve to be told as part of the First State's eerie folklore.

According to documents submitted for the Castle's nomination for the National Register of Historic Places, which was granted in 1973, the house was commissioned by Dr. Allen Voorhees Lesley in 1855. Little is known about Dr. Lesley and his wife, Jane. Their sudden arrival in Delaware is mysterious, and their lives before 1855 are largely unknown. Jane L. Lesley seems to have no biographical information at all, other than the fact that she was born in New York in 1816 the daughter of a merchant; we also know the date of her marriage in 1844 and the date of her death thirty years later. But the report nominating the Castle for historic preservation says that Dr. Allen Lesley was a native of Philadelphia, born on Vine Street in 1822:

The son and grandson of a cabinetmaker, he deviated from the family trade to take a medical degree at the University of Pennsylvania. Dr. Lesley's reputation as a surgeon was well-known: at an early date, he applied microscopy and techniques of anesthesia to the treatment of disease.... [He] *moved to* [Delaware] *after his marriage in 1844. Dr. Lesley held Democratic pro-slavery views.*

The original building plans for the Castle included two secret rooms, as any Gothic Victorian mansion should. The first secret room's entrance was concealed within a bedroom closet on the second floor of the house. The second secret room was accessible through a wall in the servant's quarters. And more than that, in the basement of the Castle, there was a hidden door that, once opened, revealed a tunnel that led directly to a nearby lake. Since all these unusual features were planned in the building of the Castle by Dr. Allen and Jane Lesley and reflected in the original blueprints, there has been much speculation over the years about what their intended purpose could have been. Was the house to be a stop on the Underground Railroad? Or, considering the pro-slavery views the Lesleys were recorded to hold, was their intent something much more sinister and frightening? We cannot know for certain, but there are things that have been whispered in the dark throughout the years that may provide a potential answer.

Jane L. Lesley died on July 31, 1874. Her husband, Dr. Allen Voorhees Lesley, died on November 7, 1881. The National Register of Historic Places nomination form for the Castle details the next part of the house's history: "Between Dr. Lesley's death in 1881, and 1903, the house remained in the hands of successive caretakers. Seldon S. Deemer...a steel manufacturer, purchased the house in 1903." An article from the *News Journal* titled "The Spirit of the House," written by staff reporter Edward L. Kenney and published on April 23, 1998, says, "But nothing explains what Deemer found shortly after he moved into the house. In a storage closet above the back stairway were two skeletons, one male and one female—shackled together. The remains were buried somewhere in Dover."

In 1994, the Castle was purchased by William and Elaine Class, who intended to turn it into a bed-and-breakfast. By this time, the house had been vacant for some years and needed a great deal of restoration. Together, with their daughter, Lesa, Elaine and William Class set about their work and quickly realized they were not alone in the house. An unseen presence seemed to lurk in every room, watching their activities as they brought the old Victorian mansion back to life. The mysterious doctor

"Little is known about Dr. Lesley and his wife Jane."

and his wife, it seems, were still very much in residence over 120 years after their deaths.

Author and historian Ed Okonowicz visited the Castle in 1997 and included it in the fifth volume of his Sprits Between the Bays series: *Prescence in the Parlor*. He wrote:

> *Very large, dark carved doors indicate the main entrance. Upon entering, first time visitors are amazed at the interior hall with its bright wooden floor, thick banister, and impressive size. After a brief tour of the first floor, I was escorted into, most appropriately, a magnificent formal parlor. Seated below 13-foot ceilings, surrounded by massive paintings, ornate woodwork, and crown molding, I talked in hushed tones with the inn's owners on a very cold*

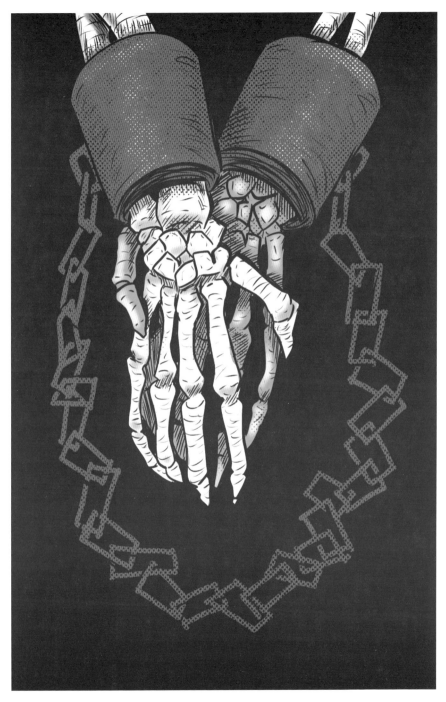

"Two skeletons, one male and one female."

The Castle. *Photograph courtesy of the Library of Congress.*

winter night. Everything was perfect. If a photograph were taken, it could have served as an opening scene from a Gothic, mystery movie. Although the ghosts did not appear on my two hour visit, rest assured they are there. Owner Elaine Class and her daughter, Lesa Class-Savage, both have seen them, heard them, and, on occasion, even felt them.

When the Classes first occupied the Castle, all the furniture was removed, so the rooms stood empty and in a state of near ruin. It took months of repair work to return the house to its former splendor. Almost immediately after they started their restoration, word quickly spread among the locals of the town that the Castle had living inhabitants once again. Those who had long lived in the town and knew the Castle's secrets did not hesitate to approach Elaine and Lesa when they were out and about with cryptic, unsettling questions and vague bits of lore:

"Have you heard the footsteps yet?"

"Be careful in the basement. That's where the doctor experimented on cadavers, they say."

"Something awful happened up in the tower room. Don't go up there alone."

Stairwell of the Castle. *Photograph courtesy of the Library of Congress.*

When pressed to provide more concrete details, these locals either did not know more information or were reluctant to share it with the new owners of the Castle. But it did not take long for Elaine and Lesa to begin experiencing this unnerving haunting for themselves after they moved in. As the intensive restoration work began, Elaine's mother, Millie, decided to help her daughter and granddaughter and moved into the house for their first month. Seventy-five years old at the time, Millie was a lifelong nonbeliever of ghosts and all things supernatural.

One night, Millie had a strange dream. In her dream, she was looking out of her bedroom window and suddenly observed a man in a navy or air force captain's uniform standing in the garden, looking up at her window, directly at her. Then with unnatural speed, the figure of the captain ran to the outside entrance to the basement and fled down the stairs, into the bowels of the house.

Neither Elaine nor Millie thought much of this dream until a few days later. As workmen were carrying many boxes of old books out of the house, one volume unaccountably slid off the top of one box and fell noisily to the floor. Upon examination, it appeared to be a handwritten pilot's log from the early twentieth century. Not long afterward, Elaine Class learned from a local historian that, for a brief time, rooms in the Castle had been rented to army pilots and that at least one of them had died in the house by suicide. While they initially thought she just had a strange dream, Elaine's mother may, in fact, have been visited by one of the mansion's many restless spirits.

Lesa Class-Savage was meant to live in an apartment on the third floor of the Castle while she and her mother did their work. But in the end, she never spent a single night there. One evening, at sunset, as she was in the process of sanding down the walls and floors to help bring them back to their original luster, Lesa caught a glimpse of a dark shadow out of the corner of her eye. As Ed Okonowicz wrote in *Prescence in the Parlor*:

> *Thinking her mother had come home, she stopped her work, looked, and found she was alone. Soon, the shadowy movement occurred again. Then she clearly heard the sound of a woman laughing.* "I got scared then," *Lesa said.* "I had the distinct impression, the feeling, that there was a woman, and it was important or urgent that I leave.….So I left."

When Lesa told her mother about what she had experienced and said that it might be best for them to not work upstairs after dark, Elaine laughed it off. She didn't believe the ghosts—if there were ghosts—would do anything to harm either of them. It didn't take long for Elaine to realize she was mistaken. A week later, Elaine and Lesa were both working on the third floor as the daylight began to fade. Lesa became filled with dread and told her mother that something wanted them both to leave. Elaine said mockingly that there was nothing "they" could do to them and left the room to get more supplies.

Just a moment later, Lesa heard her mother screaming, "Run! Run! We have to get out of here!" Elaine raced down the staircase with Lesa not far behind her. Once they were outside the house, Lesa asked her mother what happened. After taking a few deep breaths to compose herself, Elaine said that she had been standing at the top of the stairs when she felt a pair of strong hands touch her back—and begin to push. In that terrifying moment, she felt the presence of seven entities, six men and one woman, coming toward her. Elaine and Lesa never worked on the third floor after dark again.

After this incident, the haunting of the Castle intensified. Elaine and Lesa both began to hear voices in the house, whispering just out of hearing range. This happened most often on the third floor, where it sounded like a woman's voice, and in the basement, where the voice sounded more like a man. Contractors who were hired to work on specialized projects expressed to the owners that they felt uncomfortable in the house. Some of them showed up for their first day of work and then never returned. Nevertheless, Elaine and Lesa persisted in their renovations.

Then the spirits began to manifest themselves visually. Both Lesa and Elaine, independent of one another, saw the ghostly figure of a woman in clothing from a previous century peering through one of the first-floor windows. On several occasions, both mother and daughter entered the third-floor apartment to a shocking sight: a man seated in front of a roaring fireplace, dressed in white clothing, staring directly at them. When they turned away, the man in white was gone, and the fireplace was unlit. It was later discovered that Dr. Allen Lesley had used that room to see patients. Elaine and Lesa both believed the spirit of the woman was that of his wife, Jane Lesley.

In an interview with Ed Okonowicz, Elaine discussed what the ghosts looked like to them:

> [They were] *not just wispy, like a cloud, but actually having the form of a human being. It would be like seeing a motion, or seeing you, out of the corner of my eye as you passed by rapidly. Both of my cats are aware that there is something else here in the house. At times, they'll freeze,*

The interior of the Castle. *Photograph courtesy of the Library of Congress.*

and they'll stare at an area where they must see some motion or something moving.... The first question people ask when they come inside is, "Is this place haunted?" and I answer, "Yes!" They don't expect you to say "Yes." When they hear your answer, they usually have this frozen smile, and they don't say anything.

As the renovations of the Castle neared their completion, Elaine and Lesa began to sense their efforts were earning the approval of the house's unearthly inhabitants. One day, while they were on opposite sides of the third floor, they were stopped in their tracks by the clear sound of a woman's voice saying, "It's looking really good up here. It really is." And then the pennies started appearing. Whenever Lesa or Elaine would finish cleaning a room to prepare it for the next guest, they would find a penny either in the center of the bed or on the middle of the room's floor. Initially, this puzzled them, as there was no way they would have missed seeing a penny while they were going about their cleaning. The pennies seemed to appear out of nowhere, perhaps left there by ghostly hands.

Eventually, Elaine and Lesa were given an article that stated during the nineteenth century, it was a common superstition to place a penny on top of a room's doorframe or on a windowsill to prevent ghosts from entering the space. Lesa and Elaine then took the mysterious appearances of the pennies to be the ghosts of Dr. Lesley and Jane saying that while they were happy the mansion had been restored to its former splendor, there was nothing that could be done to exorcise their spirits from the place they had lived and died in. The Castle was and always will be, their house.

———•———

BUT WHO WERE DR. Allen Voorhees Lesley and his wife, Jane, exactly? That is a fact that remains largely shrouded in mystery, as very little about their lives is known. Patricia A. Martinelli, in her excellent book *Haunted Delaware*, suggests an intriguing and deeply disturbing possibility that has long been whispered about in the legends and lore of the First State. It has been proposed that Dr. Allen and Jane Lesley were not who they appeared to be— that these were assumed names and identities used to guard the two from retribution for prior atrocities they committed in the city of New Orleans years before they came to Delaware to build the Castle. We can never know for sure, but what if Jane Lesley and her doctor husband were the figures

The rebuilt LaLaurie mansion in New Orleans's French Quarter as it appeared in 2022. *Photograph by APK, Wikimedia Commons.*

known well in haunted history and true crime lore as Madame Delphine LaLaurie and Dr. Leonard Louis Nicolas LaLaurie?

The story of Madame Delphine LaLaurie was introduced to many by her fictionalized appearance in the television series *American Horror Story: Coven*, in which she was portrayed by Kathy Bates. The real story is much more disturbing. Delphine LaLaurie and her third husband, Dr. Leonard LaLaurie, lived in a grand house at 1140 Royal Street in the heart of New Orleans's French Quarter. It was there that their souls' shared love of sadism found an ideal home. Between 1830 and 1834, the deaths of at least twelve enslaved Black people were recorded at the LaLaurie Mansion. Eyewitnesses saw an eight-year-old enslaved girl, who some historians have named Lia, fall to her death from the roof of the LaLaurie Mansion, chased by a whip-wielding Madame LaLaurie, as punishment for snagging her hair while brushing it. Lia's body was buried in the garden behind the house after her death.

The LaLauries were investigated for abusing the enslaved servants in their care. According to several sources, the couple was found guilty of illegal cruelty in a court of law and forced to forfeit nine of the Black servants they enslaved. However, these liberated nine did not remain so for long. They were bought back by relatives of Delphine and Dr. Leonard LaLaurie and returned to the house of horrors on Royal Street.

On April 10, 1834, a fire broke out at the LaLaurie Mansion. It started in the kitchen and was set by an old Black woman who was enslaved by the couple and spent all her days chained to the hot iron stove by her ankle. She later told authorities she had set fire to the kitchen on purpose to kill herself, because she lived in so much fear of her cruel mistress and master's punishment. She also said that the enslaved people who were sent to the tower room of the mansion never came back alive.

The following is the report directly from the *New Orleans Bee* on April 11, 1834:

The conflagration at the house occupied by the woman Lalaurie…is like discovering one of those atrocities the details of which seem to be too incredible for human belief. We would shrink from the task of detailing the painful circumstances connected herewith, were it not that a sense of duty and the necessity of exposing and holding to the public indignation such a wretch as the perpetrator, renders it indispensable for us to do so. The flames having spread with an alarming rapidity, and the horrible suspicion being entertained among the spectators that some of the inmates of the premises where it originated, were incarcerated therein, the doors were forced open for the purpose of liberating them. Previously, however, to taking this liberty, (if liberty it can be called), several gentlemen impelled by their feelings of humanity demanded the keys which were refused them in a gross and insulting manner. Upon entering one of the apartments, the most appalling spectacle met their eyes. Seven slaves more or less horribly mutilated were seen suspended by the neck, with their limbs apparently stretched and torn from one extremity to the other. Language is powerless and inadequate to give a proper conception of the horror which a scene like this must have inspired. We shall not attempt it but leave it rather to the reader's imagination to picture what it was.

What Madame Delphine LaLaurie and her doctor husband had been doing in the dark behind closed doors at their grand house in New Orleans was nothing less than obscene Frankenstein experiments on the enslaved. In her 1945 book *Ghost Stories of Old New Orleans*, author Jeanne deLavigne adds to the tale of what was seen in the attic of the LaLaurie house in April 1834:

The man who smashed the garret door saw powerful male slaves, stark naked, chained to the wall, their eyes gouged out, their fingernails pulled off by the roots; others had their joints skinned and festering, great holes in their buttocks where the flesh had been sliced away, their ears hanging by shreds, their lips sewed together, their tongues drawn out and sewed to their chins, severed hands stitched to bellies, legs pulled joint from joint. Female slaves there were, their mouths and ears crammed with ashes and chicken offal and bound tightly; others had been smeared with honey and were a mass of black ants. Intestines were pulled out and knotted around naked waists. There were holes in skulls, where a rough stick had been inserted to stir the brains.

Less than two days after the first discovery of the fire and atrocities within 1140 Royal Street, a mob of New Orleans citizens ransacked the LaLaurie Mansion and later burned it to the ground. A house was subsequently rebuilt on the same spot, and to this day, it continues to hold a reputation as one of the most haunted places in the city of New Orleans. Madame Delphine LaLaurie and her husband, Dr. Leonard LaLaurie, fled Louisiana and escaped justice. Some say they went north and immigrated to Paris, where they both eventually died.

Or perhaps, as legend has it, they settled in Delaware and built a house called the Castle, where they reinvented themselves with new identities and continued their horrific human experiments in relative anonymity and without consequence—a mansion with secret rooms; a secret tunnel that leads to a nearby body of water; a house where, in the early twentieth century, two skeletons were discovered chained together in a closet without any explanation. Dr. Allen Voorhees Lesley and his wife, Jane, were buried in Philadelphia's Laurel Hill Cemetery. Whatever secrets their bones may hold, they took with them to the grave.

8
The Legend of the Devil's Road

Urban legends are some of the richest seams of American folklore. We seem to inherit these creepy tales from generation to generation, telling them to each other around campfires as children and then passing them on to others like a favorite story—stories best told in the dark, preferably on a stormy night, with the rain beating down on the roof, thunder echoing around you and flashes of lightning illuminating fearful young faces as you speak or listen, certain that you are all going to have nightmares.

Everyone knows a few of these tales, whether they've sought them out or not. Most of us know the story of the babysitter who kept receiving phone calls that grew more and more disturbing until the police called the babysitter and said the worst thing possible: the calls were coming from inside the house. There's also the tale of the couple who parked their car at an isolated lovers' lane and heard a radio broadcast that said a homicidal maniac had escaped from the local insane asylum. He was a killer with a hook for a hand. The girl was frightened and wanted to go home, but the boy (of course) told her there was nothing to fear. But then there was a *scritch-scritch-scriiitching* sound outside the car, and the girl demanded to be taken home. The boy got angry (what a great guy) and started the car, and then he peeled away from the lovers' lane in a rage at a very high speed. He drove the girl home without speaking to her (again, what a guy). When they arrived outside her house, he turned off the ignition and got out to open the passenger door. Instead, he fainted (brave guy), and the girl got out to see what was wrong. Hanging on the passenger door was a bloody hook.

Delaware boasts many urban legends of its own, several of which I chronicle in my first book, *Haunted History of Delaware*. There's the tale of Maggie's Bridge, located on a deserted road in Seaford, where many teenagers from time immortal have gathered at midnight to try to catch a glimpse of the ghost of Maggie Bloxom, who holds her severed head in her hands and is forever searching for her lost baby. Also in Sussex County, there is the legend of the Catman, who guarded the abandoned graves of Long Cemetery in life and continues to do so after his death, with dire consequences facing anyone who dares to roam the cemetery after dark.

When I was growing up, there was another legend that was whispered when the adults were out of earshot. It frightened me in ways the other tales didn't. It wasn't about ghosts at all but about the evil that human beings can do, which was far more disturbing to my young mind. Somewhere in Delaware, the kids would say—usually in the dark, a flashlight held under their face for maximum creepiness—there was a place called Satanville. You knew you were near it when the road you were driving on got narrower and narrower and the ancient trees overheard blocked out the sun so that it seemed like midnight in the afternoon. These were no ordinary trees; they bent unnaturally away from the road, as if they were trying to escape the abominations that occurred in the woods on the other side.

This was an unholy place: the Devil's Road. Some would say this area is one of the seven gates to hell itself. If you get out of your car and venture into the damp thickness of the overgrown forest, you will begin to see warning signs to turn back. Sometimes, these signs are literal—the words "No Trespassing" written in red paint, or perhaps in human blood. But there were other signs that this was a place you entered at your own risk: the corpses of animals slit open from throat to groin; an old, gnarled tree whose huge roots formed the shape of a skull; beheaded dolls poking out of the earth; and finally, the red pickup trucks that somehow lay in wait in the woods, ready to chase you down the road at dangerously high speeds.

However, if you somehow bravely or foolishly manage to get past all these obstacles and continue deeper into Lucifer's woods, you will find what you were looking for, the place your friends had dared you to find: the Cult House. It is an old mansion completely secluded in the forest, with window frames that are in the shape of inverted crucifixes. Legend has it that the house was originally built by the DuPont family, although no records of this exist. In old times, it is rumored, the DuPonts sometimes married close family members to keep their immense wealth secure from outsiders. Inevitably, the DuPont children who were born from these incestuous unions

"Ready to chase you down the road."

were sometimes stricken with massive deformities. These monstrous children were secluded in what is now known as the Cult House, hidden away from prying eyes as if they never existed. Stories are also told that once, a child was born so severely deformed that they were killed shortly after birth and buried under a tree near the house. Over time, the roots of the tree took on the appearance of a human skull; this is the tree often noted by travelers as they attempt to find the house.

Eventually, if the legends are to be believed, the last of the deformed children died, and the DuPont family abandoned the mansion to the forest. It was after this that the house and the entire area surrounding it was claimed by a satanic cult for its headquarters. On dark and moonless nights, the cult would gather and perform rituals to worship the devil inside

"The Skull Tree."

the old mansion. Whenever favorite animals or beloved young children from the surrounding area would disappear, it was assumed by the locals that they had been abducted by the cult and used in unspeakable rites of animal and human blood sacrifice. The road where the trees are bent away in shame became a place that was feared and avoided, except by the foolish mortals who attempted to infiltrate the grounds of the Cult House and discover its arcane secrets. At best, they would be chased away by the ferocious guardians of the grounds in their pickup trucks until they were far enough away. At worst, those who dared to enter the realm of the Devil's Road never returned.

These were the stories I heard growing up in southern Delaware, and there was never a shortage of people telling them who had another friend or a family member who had tried to find the Cult House in the dead of night. They related horrifying incidents of adventurers driving along the road when they suddenly saw headlights appear in the middle of the woods. This was unsettling, because there were no roads or paths among the trees where vehicles could hide. They would then be chased by these vehicles at high speeds for several miles until they finally reached civilization, and then, suddenly, the pursuing truck would vanish as quickly as it had appeared, leaving the thrill-seekers feeling lucky they had escaped the realm of the Cult House alive.

"The Cult House."

When I got older and started doing more research into this particularly harrowing legend, I was shocked to learn that the area known as Devil's Road is not in Delaware at all, but is in Chadds Ford, Pennsylvania, just across the northern border of the First State. The road's official name is Cossart Road, although in the present day, you will find no signs identifying it for reasons I will explain in due time. This is a tale that makes a fascinating and eerie case study of how an urban legend evolves throughout time and how its potential origin lies in real acts of horror.

Author Matt Lake, in his book *Weird Pennsylvania*, devotes a memorable chapter to the legend of Devil's Road and the Cult House. He also provides testimony from several witnesses who experienced uncanny and disturbing things. The following are a few tales from survivors of Devil's Road that were collected by Matt Lake for *Weird Pennsylvania*.

Deena Haiber said:

Here is my personal experience with "Cult House" (I have been occasionally driving by the place with friends and researching its history for about seven years now). The windowpanes actually are in the shape of inverted crosses. This seems to be not necessarily intentional—it may just be how those particular panes are shaped. The trees do grow at an extreme angle away from the house. I've never seen trees grow so off-kilter before. In some places, they do seem to grow away from the main light source. This phenomena stops once you get about a quarter of a mile past the house. There is a guardhouse, and there are red trucks. They have actually followed me before on two occasions. The first was at night, and the truck's lights were off. This is amazing, because there are no streetlights, and the trees allow in no moonlight. I couldn't understand how the driver was able to even stay on the road! I was behind it at first. The truck pulled over and waited for me to pass. It then pulled out and followed me until I was several miles from the house. I had one passenger in the car, and you can imagine the state we were in. We were scared to death, but REALLY excited! The next time was also at night but with a different friend. After we had driven past the guardhouse several times, we noticed that we were being followed by a red truck. We hadn't seen it even come onto the road. We never saw the driver's face. Again, we were followed until we were several miles from the house.... The "skull tree" does look frighteningly like a human skull. I have never found any newspaper accounts confirming that remains of any kind were found in the tree. I have been able to find absolutely no evidence of sacrificial rites being performed during Halloween or at other times, according to local records. I have also, up to this point, been unsuccessful in trying to dig up deeds, or any type of records of transfers for the property.

Brooke Meadows said:

Driving down the road toward the mansion, we noticed a pile of dead animals, mostly raccoons, slit from throat to genitals and completely gutted. It was like there was just a frame of the animal left. When we finally approached the mansion, I was even more disgusted. Hanging from the black iron gate were more carcasses like the ones we'd just seen. It's also said that if you go at night, you can hear the Satanic worshipping that goes on inside, word for word.

Stephanie said:

I have been on Devil's Road numerous times, at least a hundred. I have been up to the Devil's House. The roof is lined with metal crows all facing in the same direction, and there is a white cement bench in the front yard with a demon's face perfectly carved on it. People really do chase you out of there. I remember one time, around 2:00 p.m., I was driving with one of my friends on Devil's Road, and a black SUV sped up behind us then turned into the woods. There was no dirt road or anything; it just turned right into the woods, then the next thing I knew, he was coming full speed right towards us. One time, when there was a full moon, I could see a fire and the outlines of about twelve to fifteen people standing in a circle around it. Then I got chased off by two Bronco SUVs.

In the three testimonials I have included, you may notice that one important detail has changed. When I first heard of this legend in the 1990s, the cult members used red pickup trucks to chase intruders away from the Devil's Road. But as we move into the twenty-first century, the red pickup trucks have been replaced by black SUVs, an evolution of the legend over time to fit more contemporary relevance. It is also important to note that as the tales of the Cult House grew and became more widespread, the area surrounding Cossart Road became filled with thrill-seekers and teenagers who had a vested interest in perpetuating the legend—much the same situation as that of the lore about the Selbyville Swamp Monster in the mid-twentieth century (more about that in my book *Haunted History of Delaware*). For that legend, even my own grandmother ventured out into the darkness of the night with her friends to catch a glimpse of the creature or perhaps scare away others who came with the same mission—all in the spirit of good, clean Halloween fun.

However, there is a real horror that may well have been the unwitting genesis of the legend of the Devil's Road. It dates to 1978 and is a piece of history many would rather forget. A man named Bruce Johnston was the leader of one of the most notorious and deadly criminal gangs of the twentieth century. The gang's reign of terror began in the 1960s and lasted for nearly twenty years. The Johnston Gang members were notorious for their robberies in Pennsylvania, Maryland and Delaware. Bruce Johnston and his crew were highly skilled in picking locks, cracking safes, disarming security systems and hot wiring vehicles. They paid close attention to police scanners to stay one step ahead of local law enforcement. They would go as far as tricking state police by phoning in false reports of crimes to disguise the one they had just committed. A police officer who worked on the case later stated, "Nothing in my experience ever compared to what they were."

As the Johnston Gang continued to get away with their audacious crimes, their membership expanded. But as the circle of law enforcement began to close in on them, leader Bruce Johnston devised a plan to silence members of the gang he thought might be the most likely to testify against him in a court of law. This included what was known as the "Kiddie Gang," led by Bruce's own half-brother James "Jimmy" Johnston (eighteen years old), Dwayne Lincoln (seventeen years old) and Wayne Sampson (twenty years old). On August 16, 1978, these three young men were led to Cossart Road at night, ordered at gunpoint to dig their own graves and then shot to death and buried at the edge of the woods, where the trees now bend sideways, away from the sunlight.

Three more murders followed in that deadly month, all orchestrated by Bruce Johnston. On August 21, 1978, James Sampson (twenty-four years old) was killed. On August 30, Robin Miller (fifteen years old) was killed. Robin was the girlfriend of Bruce Johnston Jr., Bruce Johnston's son. The same day, Bruce Johnston tried to kill his nineteen-year-old son. However, Bruce Johnston Jr. survived and testified against his father in court. His father was convicted and sentenced to serve six life terms in prison. Bruce Johnston died in prison on August 8, 2002, at the age of sixty-three.

After James Johnston, Dwayne Lincoln and Wayne Sampson were murdered on August 16, 1978, their bodies were not found until December 1978. An article from the New Orleans–based *Times-Picayune* newspaper reported:

On Dec. 30, 1978, then–State Trooper Tom Cloud was on his knees digging at the frozen ground with a tablespoon in the middle of a sprawling estate in Chadds Ford. Beside him was Chester County Detective Larry Dampman. "It was a surreal scene," said Cloud, now a private investigator in West Chester. Battery-powered lights, such as the ones used in a photo studio, cast an eerie glow over the hilltop area. A bonfire was going nearby. Dozens of police milled about. Investigators scraped away dirt carefully, so as not to damage what they were looking for. Finally, resistance to the digging softened. The police had found what they were there for—and the stench was overpowering. Slowly, spoonful by spoonful, the bodies of three young men were unearthed.

The bodies of Jimmy Johnston, 18, the stepson of Bruce Sr.; Wayne Sampson, 20; and Duane Lincoln, 17, had been piled like firewood, one on top of the other. Their faces were unrecognizable. One wore a Tweety Bird shirt. The discovery would eventually break up a notorious ring of criminals that had eluded and taunted police for years. There was no jubilation, though.

"It was the most gruesome thing I ever saw," Cloud said. "And it was sad. Here were these kids with their whole lives in front of them." Dolores Troiani, who helped prosecute the Johnstons as a young assistant district attorney, remembers that the best-preserved parts of the bodies were the feet, because the boys wore heavy work boots.

"The smell was so bad. I threw away my clothes," she said.

Standing next to Troiani was Ricky Mitchell, the Johnston confederate who led police to the horrific find. He decided to inform on the brothers because if he didn't, "he knew he'd be the next one in the ground," Troiani said.

The three had been killed on Aug. 16, 1978. Mitchell had killed Sampson, the last to be shot. David Johnston had killed Duane Lincoln. And Bruce Sr. had taken care of his stepson. Later, another gang member, Leslie Dale, would tell police that Bruce Sr. told him Jimmy Johnston was still gurgling when he was dumped into the common grave.

As frightening as stories about a satanic cult practicing their dark arts in a creepy old mansion in the woods are, the story of this triple murder on Cossart Road is the true horror. It is likely that this tragic and grisly event was the spark that ignited the legend of the Devil's Road and the Cult House, as the area does not seem to have been thought of as sinister or unusual before 1978. The trees on the road are unusually bent and twisted, it's true, but some have suggested this may be because of how the trees were cut to avoid hitting the power lines. There is no definitive evidence that the Cult House really exists. With all the photographic evidence of the trees, the Skull Tree in particular, there is not a single known photograph of the Cult House, even though many have claimed to have found it over the decades. The vehicles that chase people away from the area may not be driven by cult members guarding their territory but instead by neighbors who are tired of the curious coming through their neighborhood at night, trespassing and leaving graffiti and other destruction in their wake.

Indeed, in recent years, finding the area known in legend as the Devil's Road has become more and more difficult. Neighbors had the street sign for Cossart Road removed and barriers put in place. The Skull Tree first had the areas between its gnarled roots filled with concrete, and then it was finally cut down and no longer exists. However, the urban legend surrounding this area will probably never truly die. There is something uncanny about the area made more eerie by the knowledge of the murders that occurred there. Filmmaker M. Night Shyamalan also grew up with the sinister stories of the area, and in 2004, he used the woods surrounding the Cult House as the primary location for shooting his movie *The Village*, in which a community is terrorized by figures in red robes that haunt the forest.

Of course, you never know. Perhaps there is something in those deep woods the neighbors don't want the public to know about. Perhaps there is a crumbling old mansion that only the lucky or foolish can discover, with terrible rites performed within its moldering walls at midnight on Halloween. Perhaps there really is a cult that meets there, drawn to this place by the ritualistic slaughter of three young men back in August 1978. Perhaps—but you'll never know until you explore it for yourself, right? But be warned, they might catch you in the dark, dark night. And the consequences may be severe. As I said, some who go in search of the Devil's Road never come back.

9

A Year of Terror on Route 40

For Shirley, Catherine, Margaret, Michelle, Kathleen and all who loved them.

Delaware, being one of the smaller states in the country, has perhaps been fortunate in that only two known serial killers have ever operated there. The first was in a former century: Patty Cannon, whose horrific crimes I wrote about in my previous book *Haunted History of Delaware*. But there is another who has stained the ground of the First State with innocent blood much more recently, in the latter part of the twentieth century. Like Patty Cannon before him, he was eventually caught but not before at least five women were dead at his hands over the course of one year. Although what you read in this chapter may be harrowing, I want to assure you it is not his story I want to tell as we huddle around our campfire for warmth. Instead, I want to share the story of his victims, the lives they lived before they were ended too soon, and the story of all those who helped bring the Route 40 serial killer to justice.

The year of terror on Route 40 began on November 29, 1987, a few days after Thanksgiving. It was a dark and stormy night when Shirley Anne Ellis left the warmth and comfort of her family's home just before 6:00 p.m. to bring a platter of Thanksgiving dinner food to two friends who were being treated for AIDS at Wilmington Hospital. Shirley Ellis had previously been a sex worker and arrested for it, and she had also reportedly struggled with drug addiction. But Shirley had since left the profession, stopped using drugs and was now planning on going back to school to become a nurse. But on this night, she made the decision to use her previous experience in hitchhiking on Route 40, as she knew it was the fastest way to make the fourteen-mile journey to the hospital where her friends were waiting. Shirley's sister saw her walking east along Route 40 in the direction of the big city of Wilmington, and that was the last time she ever saw Shirley alive. At some point soon afterward, a vehicle must have picked Shirley up to give her a ride. But Shirley never made it to the hospital, and she never returned home.

At 9:25 p.m. that same night, two teens who were seeking a lovers' lane were driving along Route 40 in the secluded area of Old Baltimore Pike Industrial Park, just south of the town of Newark, Delaware, when they saw what they thought was a discarded mannequin lying on the side of the road. As they got closer, they realized what they were seeing was not a mannequin but the body of a woman. The couple called 911, and New Castle County police detective Joseph Swiski went to the scene of the crime. He related what he saw in a 2016 interview for an episode about the case for the true crime television series *Grave Secrets* called "The Signs on Their Bodies":

> *She was lying at the edge of the road, approximately three feet from the curb line. She was on her back. Her pants were pulled down to her knees. Her shirt was open, and her breasts were exposed. One thing I also noticed is there was no disturbance in the ground around her, so it was like she was just dropped where she was found lying there. We found a piece of duct tape in the back of her hair. We realized the duct tape had been on her mouth. You could see that there was mutilation in her breast area. She had a mark on her stomach. She had marks on her hands. It appeared she had put up a fight with her attacker. So, on one hand, I'm seeing I have a murder, but then I'm seeing these added elements that were foreign to me. I didn't understand what that all meant at that time.*

The body of the murdered woman was quickly identified as that of Shirley Anne Ellis. Detective Joseph Swiski began his investigation into her murder, saying:

> *When you see the body at the crime scene, you're going to think she was sexually assaulted. The victim was not sexually assaulted…in the traditional sense.…Both nipples had been mutilated, and it looked like a pinching-type device had been used—basically pliers or something of that nature. There was ligature marks at her ankles and her wrists, and she had a ligature strangulation mark around her neck. Examination of her skull revealed that she had been struck in the skull three times with a*

U.S. Route 40, near Bear, Delaware. *Photograph by Dough4872, Wikimedia Commons.*

hard, cylindrical object, perhaps a hammer, with such force that it actually crushed her skull.

Kathleen Jennings, who, as of this writing, is the attorney general of Delaware, spent several decades beforehand as a highly respected state prosecutor. She became intimately involved in the investigation of Shirley Ellis's murder and those of the subsequent victims of the Route 40 serial killer. She was ultimately instrumental in bringing him to justice. Over thirty years later, the case still haunts her. Speaking about Shirley Anne Ellis, Kathleen Jennings said:

> *Someone had tortured her before she was killed. That was highly unusual and highly disturbing. I had certainly seen some gruesome murder scenes, but this one seemed very deliberate. I had never, never seen that kind of deliberate and premeditated, cold-blooded murder before.... There was no reason for Shirley Ellis to be killed. No angry boyfriend or anything that would connect a murderer to her death.... We had no leads as to the identity of the person who would have done this. What we knew was that this was sadistic, and those types of killings are rare.*

Detective Joseph Swiski later stated, "We were never able to develop a solid suspect. There just wasn't one."

Shirley Anne Ellis was born on July 2, 1964. She was only twenty-three years old when she was brutally killed on November 29, 1987. Her gravestone in Newark Cemetery was made in the shape of a large heart in red marble and engraved with her full name and her affectionate nickname in life, "Tinker." Her epitaph reads: "Beloved Daughter."

———◆———

SEVEN MONTHS PASSED WITH no leads in the murder of Shirley Anne Ellis. On June 28, 1988, Catherine Aileen DiMauro was seen walking along Route 40. She was a thirty-one-year-old divorced woman and the mother of two young children. According to the record, Catherine DiMauro had been arrested for sex work more than once by Delaware police in the previous few years. She was last seen by a witness walking along Route 40 around 11:30 p.m. The following morning, at 6:25 a.m., her body was discovered by construction workers at the site of the Fox Run apartment complex, just off Route 40. Detective James Hedrick of the New Castle County Police was one of the first to arrive at the scene. He later said in an interview:

> The morning of June 29, 1988, I was called to a construction site known as Fox Run….Upon my arrival there, I observed a female who appeared to be possibly in her early thirties. She was completely nude. You could tell right away that the individual was not killed where she was found, which means that wherever the actual crime scene was—we had no idea at that point or where to even begin to look. There were specific injuries to the breast area, the binding of the hands of the feet, all injuries that you wouldn't see in a normal homicide. All of us were familiar with…a case that had happened prior to this, and we asked them to actually come to our crime scene and see if they felt it was similar to their case in 1987.

Detective Joseph Swiski said, "When I actually saw Catherine DiMauro's body, it became readily obvious it had to be the same person." Kathleen Jennings agreed, saying, "As soon as Cathy's body was discovered, we knew we had a serial killer on our hands." Swiski added, "The investigation takes a rather intense turn when you realize you have a serial killer. We're being assured by everyone around us that you're going to have more victims."

Typically, serial killers do not stop taking lives unless they are caught, die or are imprisoned for a criminal offense unrelated to murder. After the murder of Catherine DiMauro, the media was alerted to the similarities between the two killings, and soon, the nightly news was proclaiming that there was a serial killer active in the state of Delaware.

There was, however, a very important difference in the murder of Catherine DiMauro: forensic evidence. Her entire body was covered in blue fibers of an unknown origin. Perhaps, at last, this might be a clue they could use to catch the killer. This evidence was kept secret by the police in the hopes that it may one day be used to identify the murderer of Catherine DiMauro and Shirley Ellis. The primary detectives on the case, Joseph Swiski and James Hedrick, had no experience in hunting a serial killer. For help, they went to what was then known as the FBI's Behavioral Science Unit in Quantico, Virginia, and consulted with the now-legendary John Edward Douglas, a pioneer in the art of criminal psychology and profiling. Douglas is the author of several books, including *Mindhunter* (the basis for the Netflix television series) and *The Cases That Haunt Us*, and he was also the inspiration for the character Jack Crawford in *The Silence of the Lambs*.

After reviewing the case files of the murders of Shirley Ellis and Catherine DiMauro, John Douglas offered the Delaware detectives his "profile" of the Delaware serial killer. Based on all the crime scene evidence provided to the FBI, it was concluded that the suspect was likely a white male in his twenties or early thirties who projected a "macho man" attitude in his daily life and who secretly indulged in violent pornography. He was probably a person who made a living "working with his hands" in construction or a similar trade job, because he was using tools he felt comfortable using every day for his work, such as pliers and hammers, in the murders. The gist of the FBI's findings was that this serial killer was someone "right in your backyard," an ordinary citizen, a neighbor who no one would ever suspect of being a monster.

Catherine Aileen DiMauro was born on December 26, 1956, and was murdered on June 28, 1988, at the age of thirty-one. She was buried in All Saints Cemetery in Wilmington, Delaware, ironically only a few hundred feet away from the eventual grave site of the man who took her life.

———◆———

To CATCH THE KILLER, the FBI suggested the Delaware police make the killer come to them. Detective James Hedrick said it was recommended that "we run a decoy operation. Take a female police officer, dress her in similar attire that our victims were last seen wearing, place her in similar environments and engage in similar conversation to what a prostitute might engage in." Officer Renee Taschner, after only six months on the force, accepted this dangerous job. On her nightly walks along Route 40, she wore a wire so that every conversation she had with potential clients was recorded, and she knew there were always colleagues parked close by in case she encountered any danger. Officer Renee Taschner later said:

> *I didn't really have to think long and hard about jumping into this assignment, because to me, I was a brand-new officer. It was exciting. It was something different. It was an opportunity to work on a homicide case, and that was something I'd always wanted to do. So really, it was a no-brainer. I had a gun on me at all times. I carried a handbag that had a special pocket in it, so I was able to have my hand on my gun the entire time, aimed at whoever stopped for me in case they did something.*

Richard Finner was only five years old when he unknowingly saw his mother for the last time. His mother's name was Margaret Lynn Jordan Finner, and he later said in an interview, "What I remember most about my mom's personality is she was very nice and very kind. She always seemed to be happy. I can't remember her ever being upset. I wish I remembered more." On August 22, 1988, Margaret Lynn unknowingly said her final goodbye to her children. Richard Finner said, "The night my mother left, me and my little brother were lying up in the bed, getting ready to go to bed, and my mother came up. She told us she loved us. I remember her turning off the lights as she left and telling us goodbye and she would see us later. I still see her face saying, 'Goodbye.' It definitely just seemed like a normal night. But it wasn't. And I'll never get to see her again."

What Richard did not and could not have known at the time was that his mother, Margaret Lynn Finner, made her living as a sex worker to help support her family. When Margaret Lynn did not return home the next day, her family filed a missing persons report with the Delaware Police. Detective James Hedrick was immediately alarmed, saying, "We had no reason to believe that she would simply get into a vehicle and drive off to start a new life. She had her two children, her mother, her father, and we really quickly realized she was most likely a victim."

Three months after Margaret Lynn Finner disappeared, a call was made to 911. The caller told the 911 operator, "Two hunters just pulled up in a car and they asked me to call the state police because they found a body down at the canal. They said it looks like it's been there for a while." Richard Finner then takes up the narrative: "I really do remember feeling she was going to come home. And we waited. But then, I remember seeing my grandmother crying a lot, talking to one of the detectives in our living room. So, I'm pretty sure that's when we found out she wasn't going to come home."

The body of Margaret Lynn Finner was found near the Chesapeake and Delaware Canal. It was so badly decomposed that dental records had to be used to identify her. Based on the condition of the remains, the cause of death could not be officially determined, although the signs of torture on what remained of her body did point to homicide. For the detectives investigating the case, it was clear that Margaret Lynn Finner was the third victim of the serial killer they were hunting. A huge break in the case came when a witness came forward and said he saw Finner on Delaware Route 13 climb into a blue Ford van that was driven by a white male on the night of her death. At last, law enforcement knew the vehicle they were looking for: a blue van with blue fibers within, driven by a serial killer who had taken three women's lives so far. But as Detective James Hedrick said, "the suspect is operating right under our noses, and we're missing it."

Margaret Lynn Jordan Finner was born on August 25, 1961, and was murdered on August 22, 1988, just three days before what would have been her twenty-seventh birthday. Most articles about this case say she was twenty-seven years old at the time of her death, when, in fact, she was still twenty-six. She was survived by her mother, her father and her three children. Margaret Lynn was buried in All Saints Cemetery in Wilmington, Delaware, like fellow victim Catherine DiMauro before her. Her epitaph reads: "Memories live forever in those hearts she touched."

In 1994, six years after Margaret Lynn Finner's death, her father Robert wrote and shared a poem with his family about his daughter and the impact her murder had on everyone who knew her. He called the poem "Family Feelings."

As we gaze at the heavens at a beautiful star
Your family finds comfort in knowing there you are
We pray you have found everlasting peace at last
With this thought we are able to handle the past
Your family loves you with all their heart

There will come a time when we are not apart
Until that future time does arrive
We will continue to struggle to survive.

———•———

Three women were now dead, and the police were troubled by the fact that after a seven-month gap between the murders of Shirley Ellis and Catherine DiMauro, less than two months elapsed before the killer took the life of Margaret Lynn Finner. This suggested that the serial killer they were hunting was perhaps becoming more comfortable in his routine. And despite all the on-the-ground surveillance done by Officer Renee Taschner and others, he kept eluding the grasp of justice. But now, at least, there were two concrete clues to go on: the blue fibers found on the body of Catherine DiMauro and the blue Ford van driven by a white male that a witness saw Margaret Lynn Finner get into shortly before she was murdered. However, it also became clear that the slayer of these women was becoming more creative in hiding their bodies so that they would not be found until later, causing key forensic evidence to be lost.

The police and news media issued a formal warning that women should not walk alone along Routes 40 or 13 in Delaware. But for the sex workers who depended on these stretches of road to make money to eat and support themselves and their families, what else could they do? There was no answer. In many ways, this case is reminiscent of the Whitechapel Murders that occurred in the East End of London in 1888, exactly a century prior. They are attributed to an unknown serial killer known as Jack the Ripper. During the "autumn of terror" in 1888, at least five women, Mary Ann "Polly" Nichols, Annie Chapman, Elizabeth Stride, Catherine Eddowes and Mary Jane Kelly, all sex workers, were brutally murdered by a person or persons yet unknown. All of them were human beings with lives and histories and families and friends who mourned them. Their killer will never be definitively known, but many details of the lives they lived before their horrific deaths can be known. It's all there in the historical records if you choose to look for it. That is what matters, not the speculation about who their murderer might have been. I apply that same philosophy to this chapter, as we move forward into the darkness.

Kathleen Jennings remembers: "It was a tense time, because we knew he was out there. There was the fear that, despite our best efforts, we may not be able to find this man before he struck again. This was frightening to all of us. It rocked this area and made us all question the security of the lives we lived."

On September 14, 1998, Officer Renee Taschner was walking along Route 40 in her disguise as a sex worker when she noticed a blue van pass by her seven times in the space of twenty minutes. Finally, the blue van stopped along the road, and the man inside began to speak to her. Officer Taschner recalled, "He leans over and unlocks the door and I'm standing there and I'm talking to him." This is part of the actual conversation recorded by the wire she was wearing:

> DRIVER: *I'm tired of riding around by myself.*
> TASCHNER: *Yeah? Ha Ha! You stopped. That's a start, ya know. What do you do for a living?*
> DRIVER: *Electrician.*
> TASCHNER: *How old are you?*
> DRIVER: *Thirty-four.*
> TASCHNER: *Thirty-four? You're really cute.*

Officer Renee Taschner gave her impressions in that moment:

> *We engage in conversation and in my head, I'm clicking off really what the FBI Behavioral Sciences Unit told us in terms of the profile of the person, and he's checking off every single mark. And I just knew, instinctively, that this might be our guy. And I felt very uncomfortable, because I didn't know if someone was in the back of the van that I couldn't see, so I asked him to turn the interior light on so I could see how pretty the car was. And when he did, my stomach just sank. Blue carpet was everywhere. I had my hand on my gun at that moment, but yet I still felt a sense of vulnerability that I hadn't felt with anybody else....He was different than any other person who stopped for me. It was hard to get into a conversation. He wasn't in the moment. He was looking right through me. He was very dark. You could tell he was trying to hide something, but what that something was, you just didn't know.*

The cardinal rule of Officer Renee Taschner's involvement in this case is that she never get into a car, despite the fact that she was wired for sound, armed and observed at all times by other officers parked close by. Yet here was an opportunity to see the blue carpet fibers, known as forensic evidence in the murders, for herself. In an act that can only be described as heroic, she convinced the driver of the blue Ford van to open his doors so she could feel the luxurious blue carpet and surreptitiously take a few samples to be tested against those found on the corpse of Catherine DiMauro. The driver insisted that Officer Taschner get into his van, but she refused, saying that she was feeling tired. Finally, the driver began to show signs of becoming suspicious, and he drove off into the Delaware night. The blue carpet fibers obtained by Taschner from the van were sent in for scientific analysis to see if they matched the fibers on Catherine DiMauro's body. While the police waited for the lab results to come in, they ran the license plate of the van. It was owned by a man named Steven Brian Pennell, an electrician with a wife and two children. Could this, at last, be the name of the elusive Route 40 killer?

On September 16, 1988, only two days after Officer Renee Taschner collected evidence that might prove Steven Brian Pennell was the murderer, a woman named Michelle Anne Gordon was seen by a witness entering a blue van on Route 40. She was between twenty-one and twenty-two years old, and it was known that she was a sex worker. On September 20, 1988, Michelle Gordon's body was found floating in the Chesapeake and Delaware Canal. Her injuries were consistent with those of the other victims, convincing police that she was now the fourth woman who was abducted and murdered by the Route 40 killer. One thing was different about Michelle Gordon: she had died of cardiac arrest, not a blow to the head. The autopsy revealed that Gordon had either taken or been given cocaine prior to her torture, and her body was unable to withstand the shock of the initial injuries.

Michelle Anne Gordon was buried in Wilmington's Silverbrook Cemetery and Memorial Park. The epitaph on her gravestone reads: "Our Darling— Love Forever."

Although Steven Brian Pennell was under surveillance by police during this time, he managed to trick them by coming home at night and eventually turning off all the lights in the house he shared with his wife and children. Thinking Pennell had gone to bed, the police drove away. It was only later that police discovered their main suspect was sneaking out of his home late at night to go driving along Route 40.

On September 23, 1988, only three days after the discovery of Michelle Gordon's body, Kathleen Anne Meyer's boyfriend reportedly hit her and gave her a bloody nose. She then fled her home so quickly that she did not put on socks or shoes. Kathleen Meyer was then seen by a police officer climbing into a blue van on Route 40 around 11:00 p.m., and then she vanished without a trace. The police officer wrote down the van's license plate and later discovered, too late, that it belonged to their main suspect: Steven Brian Pennell. Born on March 24, 1962, and only twenty-six years old at the time of her presumed murder, Kathleen Meyer's body has still never been found.

Of the deaths of Michelle Gordon and Kathleen Meyer, which occurred while Steven Brian Pennell was being surveilled by police, Detective Jospeh Swiski said later in an interview, "We felt totally responsible."

———•———

FINALLY, THE LAB RESULTS came back. The blue carpet fibers matched those found on the body of Catherine DiMauro. This was more than enough for law enforcement to get a search warrant for Steven Brian Pennell's van and home. While investigating the back of the blue van, police discovered bloodstains that were later found to match the DNA of both DiMauro and Shirley Ellis. Behind Pennell's home, there was a locked shed. When officers searched it, they discovered all the items that were known to have been used on the victims of the Route 40 serial killer during their torture: duct tape, pliers, a hammer, knives, needles and handcuffs. Police also found a pornographic video tape that depicted scenes of women being subjected to sadistic torture that resulted in strikingly similar injuries to those found on the bodies after death.

On November 29, 1988, exactly one year to the day after he killed his first victim, Shirley Anne Ellis, Steven Brian Pennell was arrested and placed behind bars. At his trial, Pennell pleaded not guilty and never directly confessed to killing anyone. However, the DNA evidence from Ellis and DiMauro found in the back of his van was undeniable to the jury, and this became the first trial in the United States that accepted DNA evidence as absolute legal proof. After Pennell was charged with three murders, those of Shirley Ellis, Catherine DiMauro and Michelle Gordon, the jury voted to convict him of only the first two, due to a lack of concrete physical evidence in the latter. He later pleaded no contest to the murders of Gordon and Margaret Lynn Finner. Pennell himself asked for the death penalty and received it, and he was executed by lethal injection on March 14, 1992, a much more merciful death than the ones he gave to Shirley Anne Ellis, Catherine Aileen DiMauro, Margaret Lynn Finner, Michelle Anne Gordon and Kathleen Anne Meyer. May they all rest in peace.

Detective James Hedrick and Officer Renee Taschner both witnessed Pennell's execution. Since Pennell's arrest, Renee Taschner had been plagued by nightmares, in which Pennell escapes from prison and comes to kill her. She said in an interview with the University of Delaware newspaper, the *Review*, "I looked at him with great sadness that a human being could be so cruel. I prayed for his soul as a person, not as a police officer." Hedrick attended the execution because he "hoped and prayed that he'd tell us where we could find Kathleen Meyer or at least give us a place to look. That did not happen." Despite additional pleas from Meyer's loved ones, Steven Brian Pennell remained silent on her body's whereabouts to the very end of his bloodstained life.

Kathleen Jennings, who successfully prosecuted the case and is now the attorney general of Delaware, said, "There was a very cold and evil part of him that he hid from everyone. These women were not human beings to him. They were objects for his pleasure. And I think that came across to the jury." Soon after Steven Brian Pennell was found guilty of the murders, a large bouquet of flowers arrived on Kathleen Jennings's desk. Inscribed on the card accompanying the flowers were the following words:

> *From the women of Route 40:*
> *You made us feel like human beings again.*

10

REAL FRIGHTS AT FRIGHTLAND

Isaw it from afar many times during my childhood, and it never failed to send a shiver down my spine. While sitting in the backseat of the car driven by my parents through Middletown, Delaware, in New Castle County, I saw the horrid, rotting, skeletal face painted on an old grain silo surrounded by an old farm. Deserted farmlands have been an ideal setting for many American horror movies, like *The Texas Chainsaw Massacre* in 1974, *Dark Night of the Scarecrow* in 1981 and Stephen King's *Children of the Corn* in 1984. But as my parents told me as I was cowering in the backseat as a child, what I was seeing from the road was Frightland, a haunted attraction that opened in 1996, when I was eleven years old, and has been growing stronger and more terrifying with each passing year.

Frightland has been ranked by publications such as the *Huffington Post* and *Forbes* as one of the scariest haunted attractions in America, and it has also been featured on the Travel Channel. It sits on a sprawling 1,300 acres of farmland, 350 acres of which are dedicated to no less than eight different areas of terror, including the Horror Hayride, Ravenwood Cemetery, Fear, the Ghost Town, the Haunted Barn, the Attic, Idalia Manor and the Zombie Prison. But that isn't all Frightland has to offer; there is also a full carnival area with rides suitable for the entire family, games to play and an impressive array of food options. It's basically a horror-themed amusement park, and it's easy to see why thousands of people return year after year. Frightland truly has something to please everyone during the roughly six weeks it is open to the brave souls who make the pilgrimage. Many of the staff, or "ghouls," who scare visitors silly night after night are also veterans who keep coming back every season. Some of them have been working there for over a decade. It's not uncommon for former employees to show up, their own young children in tow, ready to initiate them into Frightland's spooky magic.

In addition, Frightland has another thing going for it that many haunted attractions throughout the United States do not: it is actually haunted by not just one but several real ghosts. The farm that Frightland occupies has a long and sinister history, and sometimes, visitors and employees get scares that are not planned parts of the experience. Kyle McMahon, who has worked at Frightland for over a decade and now serves as its marketing manager, has done studious work researching the farm's truly haunted history and chronicling the strange things seen and felt by staff and visitors over time. He even had the Diamond State Ghost Investigators come out to do a full investigation of the property in 2015, and subsequently, he used much of their recorded footage to make a documentary that can now be viewed on Frightland's website. McMahon related the dark history of the Middletown farm and his own eerie experiences:

> The property that Frightland sits on was a successful farming property for hundreds of years. The owner, Clifton Davis, was a family man. Davis came down with syphilis and committed suicide in the woods on the property. Within a year, the servant's quarters burned down for unknown reasons. His daughter hanged herself in the barn, which still sits on the property two hundred years later. The family estate sold the property, seemingly wanting to get away from a land that held so much pain for them. It went through multiple owners until 1980, when the current owners purchased the land. In 1996, the owners of the land found partners to open Frightland as a fundraiser for leukemia. Immediately, the unexplained phenomena became apparent to them. Visions of a young girl were common occurrences to people who visited. Frightland staff complained of someone watching them. Many stated they felt as if someone were following them. Some would run out of the barn, refusing to ever step foot in it again. To this day, the property owner himself will not go into the barn alone.
>
> As I spent more and more time at Frightland, it became apparent to me that there was a presence there—multiple ones, in fact. Once, I was in one of the buildings working on a project. When I went to leave, the door from which I had entered had been locked from the outside. There was no one else on the property at that time. Electronics batteries drain regularly in certain places on the property—especially the barn. Hearing tapping, footsteps

Frightland. *Photograph by Jay Joslin, Creative Commons License.*

or knocking has become a near daily happening. The instances of faint voices has not been a rare occurrence either. I had always felt a "disturbing feeling" in the barn but never knew how to explain it.

The Diamond State Ghost Investigators (DSGI) were originally formed in 2005 as Delaware Ghost Hunters. The group's mission is: "To investigate the presence of paranormal phenomena and ghostly hauntings and document the presence of spirits in our everyday life through scientific and photographic evidence....DSGI's primary goal is to help everyone possible, free of charge, with their questions, concerns, or fears of spirit activity in their home or business." Over the nearly twenty years of the group's existence, DSGI has investigated some of the most haunted locations in the First State, including Fort Delaware, the Rockwood Mansion, Bellevue Hall and the Cannonball House. It has also done paranormal investigations of Fort Mifflin in Philadelphia; Pennhurst Asylum in Spring City, Pennsylvania; several sites in Gettysburg; and the infamous Trans-Allegheny Lunatic Asylum in West Virginia. DSGI "does not endorse the use of practices such as séances and Ouija boards. DSGI attempts to gather scientific-oriented information such as Infrared Thermometer fluctuations, Electromagnetic Field Measurements, and other forms of verifiable data."

It was on April 10, 2015, that the Diamond State Ghost Investigators arrived at Frightland just as the sun began to set. Since the barn is the site with the highest level of reported paranormal activity, DSGI made that area its prime focus. Almost immediately, the investigators began to receive unusual readings. Motion detectors in one area of the barn were triggered, even though there were no living beings present at the time. At the investigators' base camp outside, a roll of duct tape appeared to be thrown toward the gathered investigators by unseen hands. Then one of the seven cameras set up in the barn moved across the room by itself while all the team members were confirmed to be on the other side of the building. In the upper floor of the barn, now known as the Attic, a cluster of balloons set up by investigators moved on their own, even though the curtains on either side of them did not, suggesting that wind was not what caused the balloons to move.

Next, DSGI moved on to Idalia Manor, one of the areas of the property where Kyle McMahon has had many strange experiences over the years. While inside, a flashlight that had been placed on a table turned off by itself. The team then began to hear tapping or knocking sounds in the room that subsequently seemed to move deeper into the house, away from them. Flashlights and cameras used by the investigators began to die, even though the batteries had been fully charged, and a sudden drop in temperature was noted. One person felt her hair being touched when she was standing by herself. But whatever was haunting Frightland saved one last scare for McMahon:

> As we had ended the investigation, I was doing my safety walk through before I locked the attic of the barn. I was using my video camera for light, as my cell phone battery had long since died. Myself and Christina from DSGI were exiting the door when I felt something hit me and then we heard a loud metallic noise. We looked down and realized it was the toy truck that we had used during the investigation and had left in a room far from the exit. We both screamed immediately and jumped out of the door. It was the clearest proof to me that the stories throughout the years were all true. It was as if that presence was saying, "Don't forget to take this back."

After reviewing all the camera footage and scientific readings from the night of the investigation, DSGI's official statement was: "The property at Frightland in Middletown, Delaware, has events and occurrences that cannot be explained."

—◦—

THE AREA FRIGHTLAND OCCUPIES is owned by Nick and Denni Ferrara. In 1996, Nick, who had long been a fan of haunted attractions, decided to create and open his own. Its first year was small, but it soon expanded, largely thanks to the help of Phil Miller, who serves as Frightland's creative director. In 1997, the Ferrara's daughter was diagnosed with leukemia (now in remission), but ever since then, a huge portion of the financial proceeds of each year's haunt, including 100 percent of the parking fees paid by its visitors, are donated to the Leukemia Research Foundation of Delaware. Miller takes great pride in the fact that Frightland does not rely on actors dressed up as famous movie monsters or slasher villains for its scares. Instead, the Frightland team has created its own unique backstory that is woven throughout all eight attractions, with several nods to the real haunted history of the farm's past sprinkled in.

The Frightland mythos, as described on its website, goes something like this: Dr. Jacob Idalia and his family moved from Tombstone, Arizona, to the area that one day became known as Middletown, Delaware. Jacob moved to a mining town near the manor house built by his son Thaddeus, who was also a doctor. Caught up in the greed and frenzy of the gold rush, outlaws set fire to Jacob's home, killing his wife and two daughters. Fueled by grief and revenge, Dr. Jacob Idalia poisoned the town's well, killing the entire population, including himself. Now, the town's spirits roam what is now known as the Ghost Town. Meanwhile, Jacob's surviving son, Dr. Thaddeus Idalia, encountered more tragedy when his beloved daughter Isabella hanged herself in the barn. Thaddeus discovered her body and slowly went mad, performing unholy experiments on humans and animals with the goal of discovering a way to resurrect the dead. Many of his unfortunate subjects died in the process of the experiments and were buried in the private Ravenwood Cemetery on the property. Others who became violent were locked away in a prison built by Thaddeus, while some escaped and lurked in the woods surrounding the farm. After Dr. Thaddeus Idalia died, some of his living experiments reclaimed the land as their own and are now looking for human victims. The cursed land is also infested with the phantoms of those who were killed, including the specters of Dr. Thaddeus Idalia and his mournful daughter Isabella—and they are all waiting for you in the dark.

Such a detailed backstory is unusual for a haunted attraction, especially since it encompasses all eight areas of the Frightland experience. I think this is one of the many superlative facets of what makes Frightland truly great. You aren't just wandering through a building being scared by actors, you have an entire history that explains, in detail, why they are there, which adds to the creepy atmosphere immeasurably. While all this information is on Frightland's website, you can also find video screens in the waiting area of each attraction that relay this information. There is also a prescribed order in which to experience the attractions. This way, the story builds on itself as you go through.

Since I wrote about the exemplary Haunted Mansion dark ride at Funland in Rehoboth in *Haunted History of Delaware*, I knew from the beginning of writing this book that I wanted to include a chapter on Frightland, which is just as iconic as Funland. The only thing was that I had only seen Frightland from a distance; I had never actually been there. I'm actually a bit of a scaredy cat when it comes to haunted attractions—as surprising as that might seem. But I have enjoyed the ones I've visited in the past, and this was for research. I definitely wasn't going alone, however. My partner doesn't like loud noises or people jumping out and touching him, so he was out. Fortunately, my best friend, Ryan, was up for the adventure.

My first visit to Frightland was on October 27, 2023. I will say that if you have the funds to spring for the VIP FrightPass tickets (which allow you to skip to the front of the lines), do so, especially if you go the weekend before Halloween like I did. My friend and I got through the eight areas of Frightland in about ninety minutes, but as we were leaving, I heard other visitors saying it had taken them three hours. Frightland is an extremely popular destination during the spooky season for a very important reason: it's incredibly good. But I can say that being able to go from one haunt to another almost immediately was a huge plus that added to our enjoyment—there wasn't any time spent waiting in a very long line to break the terrifying spell.

I won't give you a description of everything I experienced during my time in Frightland, since it's best to go in not knowing what is going to happen to you. However, I will share a few parts that have stuck with me—and perhaps given me a subsequent nightmare or two. When you first enter Frightland, you are a part of a large group that is corralled into an enclosed area, where you sit on wooden benches on either side of the space. The staff explains the rules, of which, the most important is: "Don't touch my ghouls!" And then the staff member leaves, closing the door behind them and locking you all in. Immediately, you are a bit unnerved. After a few moments, another door opens, and you are led to your seats at the first attraction: the Horror

The author at Frightland.
Photograph by Ryan Walter.

Hayride. Now, I've been on many haunted hayrides in my day, but none of them prepared me for the one at Frightland. It takes you through a winding one-mile-long journey through the farmland and then into the woods, where all manner of ghouls and ghosts await you. To be honest, for me, the hayride alone was worth the price of admission—it's that impressive. I would have been entirely satisfied if that was all Frightland had to offer, but there were still seven more haunts to go.

The Barn and the Attic were, for me, the scariest parts of all. Knowing that those areas are also the most haunted parts of the property played a part in my fear, and I'm sure that's intentional. You can feel that you are in an old structure, not one that was built just a decade or two ago. It's a building with a history—and a very dark one at that. This is literally the case when you enter the Attic portion, which has no light in it whatsoever. Throughout the entirety of the attic, it is pitch black. You can't see anything—not the hand in front of your face, not where you're going or anyone or anything that might be hiding in the blackness, waiting for you to pass by. At one point, I heard a woman's voice whisper in my ear, "Please, go away!" Was it an actor, or could it have been the ghost of the woman who died by suicide in that very spot over a century ago? I'll never know for sure, but I sure am glad I made the choice to use the bathroom before entering the barn.

Idalia Manor is the classic haunted house setting—and one of the best I've ever been through. You are let into the manor in very small groups, so it feels like you are exploring the rooms and corridors nearly alone. The crowd control by the staff was one of the hallmarks of Frightland for me, because you never felt like you were in a sea of people once you were inside any of the haunts. Some of the other haunted attractions I've visited should take notes. The set and prop design in Idalia Manor is evocative and extraordinarily creepy. In fact, in every aspect of the site, you can see the loving and skillful attention to detail its creators bring to every corner of every space. I immediately wanted to go through it all again, just so I could take a longer look at the intricacies of Frightland's world. The manor also gave me my biggest scare of the night. In one of the rooms, a decayed nursery, what appeared to be a large china doll sat on a bed. The lights flickered, and I swore its head had moved to look toward me. The lights flickered again, and it was on the other side of the bed. I started to leave the room when the lights flickered a third time. Turning around, I saw the doll was now standing right behind me. I screamed, "Oh my god, it's a PERSON!" and ran. Whoever that actor was that night, I tip my hat to you. You got me good, and I loved every second of it.

Finally—and sadly—there was only one haunt left, the Zombie Prison. I found it, in many ways, as unsettling as the Attic—but for the opposite reason. In the Attic, you're moving through total darkness. In the Zombie Prison, there is light, but you are also moving through rooms that are completely shrouded in fog. My friend and I were following two parents with their young son. Suddenly, I realized I had no idea where I was or where anyone else was. All I could see was the white fog. I couldn't see anything about the dimensions of the room I was in or where to go. I was utterly lost in the mist, and my friend and the family we were following had vanished. And then the worst possible thing that could happen in such a moment happened: I heard heavy footsteps walking behind me—*thud, thud, thud*—getting closer and closer. I started shaking and screamed my friends' name, "Ryan!" I heard him say, "Over here," from somewhere up ahead and to my right. At last, that was a direction to go in, so I ran and eventually found him. It was an incredible moment of true fear and dread that I will never forget.

After we made our escape from the Zombie Prison and its horde of undead inmates, my friend and I caught up with the family who had gone through slightly ahead of us. Now, out of the fog and into the clear, cool air of an October night just before Halloween, I could see the kid for the first time. He looked to be about eight years old at most, and in my head, I wondered how someone that young would react to all the horrors Frightland has to offer. Just after I had that thought, I heard his mother ask him, "Well, buddy, what did you think?" There was a little pause as the boy gathered his thoughts, and then he uttered an answer I agreed with wholeheartedly: "I loved it! I loved it all!"

Epilogue

A HOST OF DELAWARE GHOSTS!

There are many places in Delaware with chilling ghost stories that have been told throughout time attached to them. While some may not boast tales long enough for a full chapter of their own, they are integral parts of the First State's eerie lore. To send us off into the night, here are a few bite-sized haunts to read about before you go to sleep.

The first is an old story that was collected by Dorothy Williams Pepper in her 1976 book *Folklore of Sussex County, Delaware.* Although it is long out of print, this book is an essential volume that documents both the superstitions and everyday lives of southern Delawareans. If you can find a used copy, it is worth the price, and I hope that someday, the book will be reprinted so it can be enjoyed by new generations. Until then, there is this story, which Pepper called:

THE HAUNTED HOUSE OR SUSSEX "HANT"

West of Bridgeville was an old house said to be haunted. For that reason no tenant could be induced to stay there. It was said that when you were sound asleep a wraith appeared and snatched off the bedclothes. If, by chance, you were able to go to sleep, the same thing happened all over again. At last the landlord in desperation offered the farm rent free for a year to anyone who would live in the house. The man who took up this offer swore he feared neither man nor devil, and it was he who broke the spell. When, on the first night, the bedclothes were snatched away, he sprang out of bed and confronted a shadowy form near the door. He had furnished himself with a piece of chalk and with this hurriedly inscribed a circle on the floor into which he sprang, made the sign of the cross, and in a loud voice cried out, "In the name of God, come forth and say what you want!" Whereupon a ghostly voice answered, "Light your candle and follow me."

The wraith passed through a closed door. Having lighted his candle, the man opened the same door and, following the form, descended the stairs, crossed the hall, and was led around the house to an outside cellar way. Once in the cellar the "hant" pointed to a corner and, in the same ghostly voice, said "Dig there," and vanished. After some digging the man brought up an iron pot full of gold coins. With this he bought the farm. His sudden wealth was a source of curiosity to the community, but it was late in life before he revealed its source. The explanation of this story is said to be that a miser, stricken with apoplexy, died without time to reveal the hiding place of his hoard and so was unable to rest in his grave.

Theater Ghosts at the Grand Opera House

Built in 1871 to serve as a Masonic temple, the Grand Opera House in Wilmington, Delaware, is a masterpiece of Second Empire architecture. Many Masonic symbols were incorporated into the design of its impressive façade, most notably the Eye of Providence, which we see every day on the back of the one-dollar bill. That powerful symbol is located on the front pediment of the building, which, over time, has been affectionately nicknamed the Grand Lady of Market Street.

Theaters are ideal places for ghosts. Imagine all the passion and toil that has gone on within the walls of an old auditorium of actors, singers, directors and stage crew all working together to produce a show that will thrill and entertain their audience. The sounds of those voices, along with the avalanche of applause, still echo through the centuries. Many theaters all over the world are haunted, and Wilmington's Grand Opera House is no exception. Many who have walked its stage or worked behind the scenes have reported incidents that cannot be explained by natural means. And the building is not haunted by just one spirit—but many.

The Grand Opera House. *Photograph by McGhiever, Wikimedia Commons.*

An article by Mark Fields from *Out & About* titled "Strange Delaware," published on September 28, 2018, contains interviews with several people who have experienced the ghosts of the Grand Opera House firsthand:

> *Head Custodian Chaka Hollis has encountered a number of unexplained phenomena while on duty cleaning after shows: mop buckets moving from where they were placed, flickering lights in empty rooms, furniture inexplicably turned in another direction. The most disturbing incident involved a floating lightbulb. "We were changing a burned-out bulb in a ceiling fixture in Copeland Hall and couldn't get it loose," says Hollis. "After several tries, we gave up. Then, the bulb unscrewed itself and floated...slowly...almost to the ground. Then, it dropped the last few inches and shattered with a loud pop. It was really scary." Hollis says that he is often aware of unexpected shadows and movement in*

the historic opera house when he's the only one there. "I have learned to announce myself to the building. I say who I am and what I am doing, and then they're fine," he says.

Master electrician Genevieve Fanelli has experienced three different apparitions inside of the walls of the Grand Opera House, one of which is a malevolent presence of the third floor: "I don't know much about him," she said. "He's male, and he's pissed. I avoid that area at night and just go another way." Fanelli goes on to relate that "More than 10 different road crew members over the years have asked me who the woman in the balcony is," she says. "They see her just sitting there in period garb. I say good night to her every night as I leave, because if I don't something usually goes wrong the next day. I think of her as the spirit of The Grand itself." And then there's Tom, a specter who inhabits the chair on the left in a lobby outside the Masonic offices. Fanelli has sensed him out of the corner of her eye, but he avoids being seen. She asked around to understand who or what he is. "Apparently," she explains, "there was a former secretary for the Masons who would leave the office every night and sit in that specific chair before going home, sometimes falling asleep there for hours. He doesn't like people being in the lobby, but I acknowledge him now, and he's much nicer.

So, the next time you go see a show at the Grand Opera House in Wilmington, keep your eyes and ears open. You may encounter one of its many resident spirits from the past.

Permanent Guests of the Delaware City Hotel

Hotels are places where we like to believe we are safe. After a long day of travel, there is nothing more comforting than checking into a room for the night, knowing there is a clean bed and peaceful sleep ahead of you. However, this comfort can sometimes be an illusion. Many people have passed through these rooms before you over the years, and some guests may have checked in but never checked out, preferring to stay—forever. The Delaware City Hotel is one of these places, and the town it sits in has been called, by some, one of the most haunted towns in the state.

The 1938 book *Delaware: A Guide to the First State* describes the history of Delaware City:

Delaware City is a river town of broad, tree-shaded streets, old brick hotels that have been closed as such for decades, and one of the most charming waterfronts in Delaware. On lower Clinton St. the row of stores of varying heights, built in a solid line, has not changed appreciably in 40 years. A few small boats of shallow draft lie at the wharf on the former basin of what was once the main entrance to the Chesapeake and Delaware Canal.…Delaware City superficially resembles other Delaware tidewater villages that flourished for 40 or 50 years…and then were withered by the railroad. But these places sleep peacefully, undisturbed by ambition. Delaware City is different. There is always, going on in the vicinity, or planned for the future, some large undertaking that may restore prosperity.

This description of Delaware City largely holds true today. Built in 1828, when hope for the future prosperity of the town was at its height, the Delaware City Hotel stands tall and proud, overlooking the water's edge. If you look closely, you will be able to see the stony structure of Fort Delaware on Pea Patch Island from the coast. As I wrote in my first book, Fort Delaware is hugely haunted itself, and there have been many sightings of spirits wearing Civil War–era uniforms in the area between the water at the hotel. It was a popular watering hole for off-duty officers in its day and is also located on the shore that many escaped prisoners from the fort risked their lives to reach. Many of them failed and drowned in the icy water, but they continue to make themselves known as supernatural presences, still searching for freedom, even in death.

In the present day, the Delaware City Hotel is most known for the restaurant that occupies its first floor, which has the amusing name Crabby Dick's. The restaurant's crab cakes are some of the tastiest I've ever eaten, and it's a bonus that the restaurant embraces its resident ghosts. They even sell a T-shirt in their gift shop that reads "Spooky Dick's: Scared Stiff!" It helps to have a sense of humor about your business being haunted.

Crabby Dick's and the Delaware City Hotel building it occupies, is co-owned by John Buchheit and Dale Slotter. At first, they described themselves as firm nonbelievers in the paranormal, but after spending time in the nearly two-hundred-year-old structure, they quickly changed their minds. Their original plan, in addition to starting and running the restaurant, was to live in rooms on one of the upper floors of the building, the long-abandoned rooms of what had once been the hotel. They slept there for one single night and then never did so again. In a video interview with

Delaware City Hotel. *Photograph by Smallbones, Wikimedia Commons.*

Delaware Online News, Buchheit and Slotter elaborated on their personal experiences of the hotel's phantoms:

> *When we came up here, it was like, "This is it! We're going to rehab this and we're going to live here." And here it is, six years later....The previous owners talked about stories in this room, that guests wouldn't even stay the night in here. The stories we had heard, they would see, like, figures of a woman. They would constantly hear stuff, they would hear things, noises....And of course, it's an old building, so you can attribute it to that but...doors would open and kind of close. It's spooky.*
>
> *The first night we bought the hotel we were up on the third floor, and I had this dream. It was one of those dreams that you felt you were in, and I woke up petrified.* [The dream] *was about this chambermaid, and she was telling me to get out of the building. And I was like, "I bought the building, it's going to be mine." And then we got into a big argument, and we came to a truce in the dream. She was a maid back in the 1800s and she was all dressed up like that.* Psychic Detectives, *the TV show that's*

on Court TV, they did—not related to our building but they did a filming out on the Delaware—and they brought a psychic, Nancy Myers, in here. And I started telling her that the building has myths about being haunted, and she looks up at me and goes, "That's not a myth." And she described the woman to me, and she said her name was Sandy.

[The previous owner of the building]—he grew up in the hotel. His mother inherited it, and he grew up in it. He said that one day he was walking up to the second floor and right at the top of the steps was this woman. And he looked at her. And he turned away and turned right back, and on the second glance, she was gone. And he said it was just so real, so evident, that someone was there.

Those who work at Crabby Dick's on the first floor of the former Delaware City Hotel have grown used to the ghosts over time. They are now accustomed to seeing black shadowy figures moving out of the corner of their eyes, the sound of footsteps echoing in parts of the building where no one should be, furniture and table settings being moved around by invisible hands. For them, Sandy, the phantom chambermaid from the nineteenth century, has made it clear to all that she is very much a permanent part of the staff.

The Curse of Edgar Allan Poe

Another famous haunted inn and watering hole is the Deer Park Tavern, located in Newark, not far from the University of Delaware. The site where the Deer Park Tavern now stands was originally the home of the St. Patrick's Inn, built in 1747. The walls of St. Patrick's were witness to many notable events and important figures from history. In 1764, the inn was the Delaware home base for Charles Mason and Jeremiah Dixon, who, along with their team of surveyors, created what became known as the Mason-Dixon line, a land demarcation that would, in the following century, be used to determine the boundaries between "free" and "slave" states. During the American Revolution, it is said that soldiers, including none other than General George Washington, who fought for the Patriot cause stayed for a night at the St. Patrick's Inn.

Despite these illustrious guests, there is one other whose time at the St. Patrick's Inn has inspired notable attention in the haunted history of

Delaware: Edgar Allan Poe. The website for the Deer Park Tavern relates this anecdote:

> *On December 23, 1843, Edgar Allan Poe lectured at the Newark Academy. As he was attempting to descend from a carriage at the Inn, he was reputed to have fallen in the mud and was so upset that he put a curse on the building. "A curse upon this place! All who enter shall have to return!" Patrons found this so amusing that they carried Poe into the tavern with a hero's welcome.*

Legend has it that Poe wrote part of his immortal poem *The Raven* while staying at the St. Patrick's Inn, which he returned to once more in 1849, not long before his mysterious and premature death. The St. Patrick's Inn was subsequently destroyed by fire. In 1851, the Deer Park Tavern was built on the same spot and has remained open ever since. Its logo is, with a nod to its history, a raven. Although not conclusively verified, there are many anecdotal tales that suggest the Deer Park Tavern's basement was a stop on the Underground Railroad, sheltering enslaved Black men and women as they journeyed toward freedom in the northern states.

Deer Park Tavern. *Photograph by Pubdog, Wikimedia Commons.*

With so much incredible history within its walls and on its land, it's no surprise that the Deer Park Tavern is haunted by spirits from the past. Staff members who work there have reported hearing sounds of disembodied footsteps on the stairs, laughing and coughing in rooms where no living being is present and phantom voices. Barstools will sometimes drag themselves across the floor, as if they are being pulled by invisible hands, or they will fall over suddenly when no one is near them. Perhaps the most unsettling occurrence is when the front doors to the tavern swing open and then close, as they usually do whenever a customer enters the building, but there is no one there—at least not a patron who is still among the living.

Perhaps it's the ghost of Edgar Allan Poe, doomed by his own curse on the building, who returns again and again to the Deer Park Tavern for one final drink before last call at midnight.

A Voodoo Priest Buried in Belltown

Belltown is a small, unincorporated community located in Sussex County, not far from the towns of Lewes and Rehoboth Beach. It was established in 1840 by Jacob Bell, who is called, in historical records, a "free colored man." Belltown was one of the first communities in Delaware to become an independent entity, primarily composed of Black men, women and children. Its historical significance is immeasurable, as it remained a safe and culturally vibrant community for the Black population of Sussex County well into the twentieth century. Historically, Belltown was also a source of curiosity for its white neighbors, as written in the 1938 Federal Writers' Project book *Delaware: A Guide to the First State*:

> *BELLTOWN (population 300 est.) is an all-Negro village, with a school, church, stores, and a beauty parlor. Some of the houses shine with paint or whitewash and have well-swept front yards of bare earth.…Other dwellings are paintless tumbledown shacks surrounded by tin cans and refuse. Nearly every family has a flock of chickens or a pig or two. The village has no governing body of its own, but the people sometimes gather in the schoolhouse to discuss a problem that is affecting them.…In the mornings, most of the adult population leaves on foot or in old automobiles for Lewes or in the nearby apple and peach orchards. At night, files of Negroes, sometimes singing, plod home to Belltown—a procession that is a century-old ritual.*

It was also reported by the authors of the Federal Writers' Project in 1938 (most of whose interviewers were white, it must be said) that Belltown also became known for its so-called Devil Worshippers, a cult led by a man named Arnsy Maull. A man, according to the authors of *Delaware: A Guide to the First State*, "whose Voodoo art is still remembered and probably still followed to some extent." The book continues the tale of Arnsy Maull:

> *His clientele included Whites as well as Negroes for miles around. His "conjures" had the required power, it is said, to cure a misery or kill an enemy. The "Devil Worshippers" had a prolonged initiation period: a neophyte had to spend seven Sundays in the woods in solitary communion with the Devil, who on the seventh Sunday took possession of his soul and gave him supernatural powers.*

According to legend, on his deathbed, Arnsy Maull renounced his powers of witchcraft. The tale says he ordered his remaining followers to procure leather whips and to slash them through the air as hard as they humanly could. All the while, Arnsy Maull screamed, "Drive off the devil! And let the Lord in!" The remaining devoted to this Voodoo priest cast whips through the air until midnight and cried out prayers for his survival. But instead, Arnsy Maull gurgled out his last beath. At the same moment, a violent storm began, with thunder that seared eardrums and lightning that blinded eyes.

The body of Arnsy Maull was buried in Belltown. In 1938, Maull's son Silas said he did not believe in the devil. All he did was create "charms and cures made of herbs and other things" and continue to serve the community needs of Belltown, as his father had before him. Some say that the magic he practiced was handed all the way down into the twenty-first century.

Sometimes, they say, on dark and stormy nights, at the witching hour, you can hear the ghost of Arnsy Maull screaming to drive away the devil above the whipping of the wind.

———•———

OH DEAR, IT LOOKS like our campfire is about to go out—just enough time for one more tale before we must find our own way home through these eerie Delaware woods. One more scary story before we can go to sleep. Just one more and then on to sweet dreams.

The Many Phantoms of Abbott's Mill

When I was a child growing up in Sussex County, attending East Millsboro Elementary School, field trips were a rare treat. One place we went to on several occasions was Abbott's Mill, located in the town of Milford, Delaware. As a youngster, I looked forward to these visits with great relish. It is a beautiful place, deeply immersed in nature and filled with history. But even then, as young as I was, I felt there was another side to this place that got me out of school for an afternoon. Walking through its grounds or being inside the mill itself, I felt there was something else inhabiting the space that I couldn't see but could feel deep in my bones, lurking just outside my vision. As an adult, while doing book events throughout the state of Delaware, in question and answer sessions, the ghosts of Abbott's Mill were brought up more than once. As I did research for this book, it turned out that my childhood instincts were correct; Abbott's Mill and the land surrounding it is haunted by many phantoms from the past that refuse to leave.

The National Register of Historic Places nomination form for Abbott's Mill tells its story:

> *Abbott's Mill is a well-preserved example of a late nineteenth century/ early twentieth century milling complex....There has been a gristmill at Abbott's Pond since 1808. Before that, there was a sawmill at the site built by Nathaniel Whiley in 1795. The foundation of the present mill is likely to date from 1808, but the superstructure was rebuilt. The mill was in operation until 1960, and its flour was known to be some of the best in the area. The last miller, Ainsworth Abbott, bought the mill in 1919. It is his name which the mill and the millpond carry.*

The mill and the house are home to several restless spirits. William Johnson, who owned the mill in the early nineteenth century, died in a second-floor bedroom of the house. Ever since then, people who have dared to sleep in that room have reported the uneasy feeling of being watched by an invisible presence. Subsequent owners decided to conduct a séance to try to communicate with Johnson's ghost and implore him to move on. The medium was successful in making contact, but apparently, William Johnson was firm in that he loved Abbott's Mill and planned to remain there for eternity. In both the house and the mill, at night, lights tend to turn on and off by themselves when the structures are empty of any living inhabitants. Some say that during the time of slavery, the mill was a well-known stop on

Abbott's Mill. *Photograph by Smallbones, Wikimedia Commons.*

the Underground Railroad. This made it a target for notorious killer and slave trader Patty Cannon and her gang during their reign of terror. Legend has it that one of the Black men the gang attempted to capture and sell managed to break away and run into the woods surrounding the property, only to be shot dead by one of Cannon's nefarious crew. His ghost can be heard to this day, running through the trees by Abbott's Mill.

Visitors will sometimes hear the sound of someone pounding on the doors of the mill from the inside. Looking through a window, they can see a man in what appears to be a gray uniform inside of the mill, trying to get out. Alarmed, they find the nearest staff member and explain that a man has been locked inside the mill. However, when the staff member unlocks the doors and opens them, the mill is deserted and quiet. It is thought that the apparition of a Confederate soldier has been trapped at Abbott's Mill, although how or why his spirit came to this place is unexplained. The pond on the property has its own resident ghost as well, a young boy who is said to have drowned there over a century ago. His phantom appears mostly to other children who visit the site, and sometimes, he is heard giggling while water on the pond is made to splash upward by small, unseen fingers. Apparently, the boy was playing in the pond before he fell into it and perhaps does not realize he is dead at all.

The final legend about Abbott's Mill is perhaps the most frightening of all. On October 27, 1945, a resident of Milford was driving past Abbott's Mill Pond on his way home. He suddenly noticed a young woman standing by the side of the road, wearing a white dress. She appeared to be soaking wet, which the man found strange, as it had not been raining that night. The man stopped his car and asked the woman if she needed a ride home. The woman did not speak but nodded her head while keeping her eyes lowered. He opened the door to his pickup truck, and the woman climbed in. Seeing that she was shivering with cold, he gave her his jacket, which she gratefully wrapped around her shoulders. Still saying nothing, she pointed at the road ahead. The man started his vehicle and began driving forward. As they drove toward the town of Milford, he asked the woman why she was at Abbott's Mill Pond alone so late at night. The woman did not answer him; she only stared straight ahead into the dark. Finally, as they reached town and began to pass by houses, the woman finally spoke but said only one word: "Home."

The man stopped his truck and got out to open the passenger door. When he did so, he saw that the woman was gone. He looked around in disbelief. There was no way she could have gotten out of the vehicle and into the house in the time it took for him to walk around to the passenger door. At first, the man thought that perhaps he had imagined the entire thing; he was coming off a twelve hour shift and was exhausted, so maybe his mind was playing tricks on him. But when he looked down at the seat where the young woman had been sitting, he saw that it was still damp, and the floor where her feet had rested was stained with mud. Looking back at the old house once again, the man shook his head and decided it was time for him to go home. He had no use for the supernatural, but that night, he found himself beset by bad dreams.

The following morning, the man was getting ready for work when he realized his jacket was missing. Where could it be? Then he remembered the young woman from the night before and that he had given her his jacket. She must have been still been wearing it when she got out of his truck and ran into her house. On his way to work, the man drove back to the house where the young woman lived. He knocked on the door, and after a minute or two, it was opened by an old man who looked him up and down with suspicious eyes. "Help you?" the old man asked. The trucker explained that he had given the old man's daughter a ride home the previous night and forgotten to get his jacket back. The old man's face filled with a mixture of fury and anguish. "Why can't you all just leave me alone? Every year someone decides to play tricks on an old man with a broken heart, and it ain't nice. It ain't nice at all!"

The trucker explained he didn't mean to cause any offense; he just wanted his jacket back. Could the old man ask his daughter to bring it to him? The old man's eyes filled with tears. "She can't do that. She can't do nothin'. My daughter's been dead for ten years now. Got herself mixed up with a no-good fella who broke her heart. They found her floating in the pond at Abbott's Mill. Did away with herself, the police told me. Only sixteen years old. I put roses on her grave every year on the anniversary of her death, did it last night. She's buried out in the Odd Fellow's Cemetery. Every year, someone comes here foolin' me, saying they seen her. It's cruel. You should be ashamed of yourself!"

With that, the old man slammed the door in the trucker's face. Later that day, after work was done, the man decided to walk out to the Odd Fellows Cemetery. It wasn't far from where he lived. He wasn't sure why he was doing it, but maybe he could find the grave and see for himself. As the sunlight began to fade toward evening, the man saw a grave with an angel statue on top and what looked like a bouquet of roses beside it. He walked slowly toward the grave and stopped short when he reached it, feeling his blood turn to ice in his veins. Lying on the ground in front of the tombstone was his own jacket, neatly folded up.

The man picked up his jacket and found himself trembling. And then he heard it, he was sure he heard it—the voice, her voice, carried like a whisper on the wind: "Cold…I'm so coooold."

He ran all the way home.

The man could never bring himself to wear that jacket again. He kept it hanging in the back of his closet and tried to forget about what had happened. But once in a while, usually around Halloween, the man would take the jacket out of the closet and tell his children its story. And as the years passed, he told his grandchildren the story of how, one night, many years ago, the jacket was worn by the vanishing ghost of Abbott's Mill Pond. His kids and grandkids would listen and get spooked, but afterward, they would usually laugh and say, "But it didn't really happen, did it? It's just an old story, isn't it?"

And the man would look them dead in the eyes and say, "Sure. It's just an old story. That's all it is." Then he'd take the jacket and hang it back up in the closet for another year, seeming glad it was once again out of his sight. "Now, it's high time for y'all to go to bed. You sleep tight now, you hear?"

Later, safe under their covers, the kids would try to go to sleep. They'd listen to the wind outside the house and the tree branches scratching at the windows. And they'd feel it then—the fear begin to grow in their bellies as the old house creaked around them. Something that sounded like a footstep began climbing the stairs. Something that almost looked like a face appeared outside the window and looked in, even though their bedroom was on the second floor. They heard something like a whisper carried on the autumn breeze, the whisper of a young woman long dead now, and so cold—so awfully cold.

It's just an old story they say to themselves as they squeeze their eyes shut. It's only a story they think as they drift into an uneasy sleep. It isn't real.

But you and I know better, don't we?

Pleasant dreams, my friend.

BIBLIOGRAPHY

DeLavigne, Jeanne. *Ghost Stories of Old New Orleans*. Baton Rouge: Louisiana State University Press, 2013.

Duffy, Jim. *You Wouldn't Believe: 44 Strange and Wondrous Delmarva Tales*. Cambridge, MD: Secrets of the Eastern Shore, 2021.

Federal Writers' Project. *Delaware: A Guide to the First State*. New York: Hastings House, 1938.

Lake, Matt, Mark Moran and Mark Sceurman. *Weird Pennsylvania*. New York: Sterling Publishing Company, 2007.

Martinelli, Patricia A. *Haunted Delaware*. Mechanicsburg, PA: Stackpole Books, 2006.

Morgan, Michael. *Hidden History of Lewes*. Charleston, SC: The History Press, 2014.

Munroe, John A. *History of Delaware*. Newark: University of Delaware Press, 2006.

Okonowicz, Ed. *Spirits Between the Bays*. Vol. 2. *Opening the Door*. Elkton, MD: Myst and Lace, 1995.

———. *Spirits Between the Bays*. Vol. 5. *Presence in the Parlor*. Elkton, MD: Myst and Lace, 1997.

———. *Terrifying Tales 2 of the Beaches and the Bays*. Elkton, MD: Myst and Lace, 2001.

Pepper, Dorothy Williams. *Folklore of Sussex County, Delaware*. N.p.: Sussex County Bicentennial Committee, 1976.

Sarro, Mark, and Gerard J. Medvec. *Ghosts of Delaware*. Atglen, PA: Schiffer, 2012.

Seibold, David J., and Charles J. Adams III. *Ghost Stories of the Delaware Coast*. Wyomissing, PA: Exeter House Books, 2000.

Woods, Caroline. *Haunted Delaware: Delightfully Dreadful Legends of the First State*. Haverford, PA: InfinityPublishing.com, 2000.

ABOUT THE AUTHOR

J.R. Blackwell.

Josh Hitchens was born and raised in Sussex County, Delaware. He has been a storyteller for the Ghost Tour of Philadelphia since 2007. His first book, *Haunted History of Delaware*, was released in 2021 by Arcadia Publishing, followed by *Haunted History of Philadelphia* (The History Press) in 2022. Both books have been adapted for younger readers as part of Arcadia's Spooky America series and released as *The Ghostly Tales of Delaware* and *The Ghostly Tales of Philadelphia*. Josh is also the creator of the podcasts *Going Dark Theatre*, which examines the humanity behind the horror in true tales of ghost stories, unsolved mysteries and weird history, and *Hitchens on Horror*, in which he acts as a host for a some of the best and worst scary movies ever made. He has written articles for *Philadelphia Weekly* and the *Broad Street Review*. Josh lives in West Philadelphia with his partner and a cat named Mina.

www.joshhitchens.com

Visit us at
www.historypress.com
···